Free Will

For my mentor, Keith Lehrer, from whom
I am still learning

Free Will

Joseph Keim Campbell

polity

The right of Joseph Keim Campbell to be identified as Author of this Work
has been asserted in accordance with the UK Copyright, Designs and Patents
Act 1988.

First published in 2011 by Polity Press
Reprinted in 2011

Polity Press
65 Bridge Street
Cambridge CB2 1UR, UK

Polity Press
350 Main Street
Malden, MA 02148, USA

ISBN-13: 978-0-7456-4666-4 (hardback)
ISBN-13: 978-0-7456-4667-1 (paperback)

A catalogue record for this book is available from the British Library.

Typeset in 10.5 on 12 pt Sabon by Toppan Best-set Premedia Limited

Printed and bound in the United States by Odyssey Press Inc., Gonic, New Hampshire

The publisher has used its best endeavours to ensure that the URLs for
external websites referred to in this book are correct and active at the time of
going to press. However, the publisher has no responsibility for the websites
and can make no guarantee that a site will remain live or that the content is
or will remain appropriate.

Every effort has been made to trace all copyright holders, but if any have been
inadvertently overlooked the publisher will be pleased to include any
necessary credits in any subsequent reprint or edition.

For further information on Polity, visit our website: www.politybooks.com

Contents

Acknowledgments

Thanks to my editor, Emma Hutchinson, for the opportunity to write this book as well as for her guidance and enthusiasm throughout the process. Thanks to my colleagues, especially Michael O'Rourke, David Shier, Harry Silverstein, and Matthew Slater. Thanks to my students, especially Jason Turner. Several papers on these topics were presented at the Washington State University / University of Idaho Philosophy Colloquium series, and I thank my colleagues, graduate students, and other participants for helpful questions and comments. I've also benefited from members of the free will community, too many to mention, especially contributors to the *Flickers of Freedom* and *Garden of Forking Paths* blogs. In addition, I've profited greatly from the writings and kindness of Keith Lehrer, Peter van Inwagen, and John Martin Fischer.

Several reviewers from Polity Press gave helpful comments on my proposal. Scott Sehon, Kevin Timpe, and Manuel Vargas provided extensive, thoughtful comments on complete drafts of the book. I am indebted to each of them. Others who provided helpful comments on previous drafts are Nicole Brunson, Bob Kane, Keith Lehrer, Al Mele, Nathan Nichols, Roxanne Reese, Matthew Slater, Saul Smilansky, Kadri Vihvelin, and V. Alan White. Drafts of the first two chapters were used in several of my metaphysics classes at Washington State University. I thank all of my students, especially those who offered written comments on the first two chapters: Leslie Lambert, Juan Pena, Ross Powell, Ralph Reagan, Jaron Robinson, and Adam Sturdivant.

Last but not least, thanks to my family and friends, especially Delphine and Lake, for their love and support.

1

Free Will

This book considers various problems, arguments, and theories surrounding the concept of *free will*. We take the approach that *problems* about free will are best understood in terms of *arguments* for free will skepticism. **Free will skepticism** is the claim that no one has free will. It is the denial of **the free will thesis**: someone has free will. Given our approach, a philosophical problem is a genuine problem only if the underlying skeptical argument is cogent. It is rare that a single argument yields a result accepted by everyone. More often than not, there are various arguments lending different levels of support to related conclusions, together with a multitude of opinions about which arguments are cogent and which arguments are not. *Theories* try to make sense of it all, that is, they try to provide explanations in light of the overall evidence. We start with problems (Chs 1–2) that lead to arguments (Chs 3–4) and try to sort it out in the end by exploring a spectrum of theories about free will (Ch. 5).

My training is primarily in *epistemology*, the theory of knowledge. The central problem in that area of philosophy is the problem of *epistemological skepticism*. How do I know that I have a hand? How do I know that I'm not some handless brain-in-a-vat? As it turns out, these two skeptical problems – epistemological skepticism and free will skepticism – have more in common than one might think. A **skeptic** is one who has doubts but doubts come in degrees. The epistemic skeptic has doubts about *knowledge* and in this respect he is like the agnostic who has doubts about God's existence. The atheist has doubts about God's existence, too, but they are more extreme than the doubts of the agnostic. The atheist is a **metaphysical skeptic**, one who denies the existence of something. Free will skepticism is a kind of metaphysical skepticism, doubt reaching the level of denial. My interest in free will is connected with my broader interest in epistemological skepticism and skepticism in general. The main question for me is: Is there a good reason to doubt the existence of free will, and to accept free will skepticism?

Much of this book is concerned with **the compatibility problem**: Is free will compatible with the thesis of determinism? In this chapter, we show that the best arguments for free will skepticism include as a premise the thesis of **incompatibilism**, the view that the free will thesis is incompatible with the thesis of determinism (§ 1.5). Thus, if the free will thesis is compatible with determinism, then the best arguments for free will skepticism are unsound. This doesn't prove that we have free will but it might show that there is no good reason to deny the free will thesis, which is not an insignificant result. Before that we investigate fatalism along with other threats to freedom from time, truth, and foreknowledge (§ 1.2–1.4). But why should we care about free will in the first place (§ 1.1)?

1.1 Why Care about Free Will?

Why care if free will skepticism is true? Why care whether anyone has free will? Why should we care about free will at all? We need to know a little about free will in order to get started. In this book, we adopt the reasonable view, defended in this chapter (§ 1.2) and the next (§ 2.4), that **free will** is the power of *up-to-usness* (Smilansky 2001). In other words, the free will thesis is true if and only if some of our actions are *up to us*. We say "actions" and not "choices," for we regard choices as kinds of actions. This assumption is controversial, and arguably false. Nonetheless, we adopt the methodological approach of understanding free will in terms of free action, for it makes the subsequent discussion a lot easier.[1] Still, why care if some of our acts are up to us? Why care if any of our actions are free?

Free actions are tied up with a lot of other things about which we care, like *creativity, origination, ownership,* and *authenticity.* Views of creativity vary (Russell 2008a). Consider Michelangelo's statue: *David.* Is this a case of genuine *origination?* Was Michelangelo the *ultimate source* of the statue? Or was the statue preexistent, as it were, in the various fault lines of the marble slab, waiting for someone like Michelangelo to come along and expose it (cf. Leibniz 1704, 3)? Perhaps there can be human creativity without origination.

Some philosophers disagree and think that in order to be free, persons must be the **ultimate sources** of their actions, that is, the agent performs or even causes his free actions. Sometimes it is added that the actions have no prior causes or influences outside of the agent. These views are explored in more detail later (§§ 1.2, 3.4, 4.3, 5.1). It is undeniable that free action is required in order for us to be the ultimate sources of our actions. If no act is ever free and creativity requires origination in the sense of ultimate sourcehood, then creativity is impossible, too. Even if creativity does not require ultimate sourcehood, even if it is nothing more than the manipulation of something preexistent, it still requires free action. If *nothing* is ever up to us, then we cannot *manipulate* anything. Similar comments hold for claims about concepts like *ownership* and *authenticity* when they are applied to our actions. How can an action be *mine,* something I did, unless it was up to me in the minimal sense to manipulate it, unless it was something about which I had some control?

Free will is also important because it is presumed by many of us to be necessary for moral responsibility. Whether free will is necessary for moral responsibility is a contentious question, in part, because there is no generally accepted definition of "free will." Still, it is reasonable that if nothing is ever up to us, then no one is morally responsible for anything. Given our provisional understanding, it follows that free will is necessary for moral responsibility. Even those philosophers who deny that free will is necessary for moral responsibility believe that some kind of freedom is necessary.

The connection between free action and moral responsibility is well grounded even though there are huge disagreements about the specifics. At the end of the next chapter, we argue that our provisional definition of "free will" allows for a compromise (§ 2.4).

One might also care about free will because one is curious. There are good reasons for believing that we have free will and equally good reasons for adopting free will skepticism. It is a puzzle to see which position is more reasonable and why. Still, free will is not just a curiosity. It is an exercise in self-understanding. For those of us in the West, free will is part of our concept of *the self*.[2] Whether you're interested in the self or philosophical puzzles, or whether you think that moral responsibility matters, or creativity, origination, ownership, authenticity, or free action matter, you should think that free will matters. If you don't think that any of it matters, probably you didn't make it to this point of the book!

In the remainder of this chapter, we discuss our preliminary understanding of free will in more detail (§ 1.2). We also motivate free will skepticism with problems about fatalism, time, truth, and foreknowledge (§§ 1.2–1.5). We focus on the *problem of free will* (§ 1.5; Ch. 3), which includes the compatibility problem. What is interesting about this problem is that it remains even if determinism is false! This presents the biggest challenge to free will. If we want to show that there is no compelling reason to adopt free will skepticism, this is the place to start.

1.2 Free Will and Fatalism

Two important views about freedom and control are *monism about free will* and *pluralism about freedom*.[3] According to **monism**, all philosophers mean the same thing when they use the term "free will" (van Inwagen 2008). **Pluralists** note that the literature includes multiple and contrary varieties of freedom. Each variety of freedom is interesting and worth wanting, whether or not it counts as *the meaning* of "free will" (Balaguer 2010). For each freedom we may ask several questions. Does anyone have that kind of freedom? Is that kind of freedom required for moral responsibility? Is that kind of freedom compatible with determinism? In this book, we defend a monist view of free will but the debate is contentious and discussed throughout.

Given our preliminary understanding, free will is a *power* or *ability*, namely, the power of up-to-usness. Some philosophers believe that free will is a **set of powers**, like the powers of reflective self-control (Wallace 1994) or practical reasoning (Vihvelin 2004). Others think that free will is a single, **fundamental power** (van Inwagen 1983; Strawson 2002). According to the **classical view**, a person has free will only if he is able to do otherwise (van Inwagen 1983; Ginet 1990; Kane 1996). Most classical theorists identify the ability to do otherwise with free will (van Inwagen 1983), which entails that free will is a fundamental power.

Not everyone agrees that the ability to do otherwise is essential to free will. According to the **source view**, a person has free will only if he is the source of some of his actions, whether or not he is or was able to do otherwise (Frankfurt 1969; Fischer 1994; Pereboom 2001). Views about the nature of sourcehood vary widely, from accounts that require that the agent is the *ultimate source* – "what we do is wholly and entirely up to us in some absolute, buck-stopping way" (Strawson 2002, 451) – to others that require only that the agent is the adequate source of his action. An agent is the **adequate source** if and only if he is the source of his action but he is not the ultimate source of his action (cf. Spinoza 1677; Nadler 2009). Free will might require sourcehood yet not ultimate sourcehood.

Our provisional view is that an agent has free will if and only if his acts are *up to* him. This appears to favor the source view but it is equally acceptable to the classical view, so far as we have defined these terms. Both theorists can agree that sourcehood is essential to free will, for sourcehood is just a kind of up-to-usness. The crux of their debate lies in the acceptance or rejection of the **classical thesis**: an act is up to an agent only if he is or was able to do otherwise. Proponents of the classical view accept the classical thesis while proponents of the source view reject it. Thus, philosophers like Robert Kane, who puts an important emphasis on sourcehood, come out as classical theorists on my taxonomy since they also believe that the ability to do otherwise is essential to free will. This debate is discussed in more detail later in this book (Chs 2 and 5). Nonetheless, what's important is that discussions of free will are split between *classical theorists*, who think of it as the ability to do otherwise, and *source theorists*, who think of it as a kind of sourcehood.[4]

Free will skepticism is related to fatalism, though explaining the connection between the two is difficult. According to **fatalism**, "we are powerless to do anything other than what we actually do" (Rice 2010). We can distinguish between **global fatalism**, where *everything* we do is fated, and nothing is avoidable (Markosian 2009), and **local fatalism**, where the fatalism is less restrictive. Usually, when we think of fatalism we think of local fatalism, not global fatalism. Consider this passage from W. Somerset Maugham's play "Sheppy."

> **Death:** There was a merchant in Baghdad who sent his servant to market to buy provisions and in a little while the servant came back, white and trembling, and said, Master, just now when I was in the market place I was jostled by a woman in the crowd and when I turned I saw it was death that jostled me. She looked at me and made a threatening gesture; now, lend me your horse, and I will ride away from this city and avoid my fate. I will go to Samarra and there death will not find me. The merchant lent him his horse, and the servant mounted it, and he dug his spurs in its flanks and as fast as the horse could gallop he went. Then the merchant went down to the market place and he saw me standing in the crowd and he came to me and said, Why did you make a threatening gesture to my servant when you saw him this morning? That was not a threatening gesture, I said, it was only a start of surprise. I was astonished to see him in Baghdad, for I had an appointment with him tonight in Samarra. (Maugham 1931, 298–299)

In this example, the servant tries to escape by fleeing to Samarra only to find Death waiting there. The servant's death is unavoidable yet not everything is fixed.

For instance, that the servant dies is fated but presumably it is not fated when, where, and how the servant dies. He could have died in Samarra at some later time, or he could have died at the market. It is most natural to interpret Maugham's passage as a tale about local fatalism. It is fated that the servant die, but not when, where, or how. There might be a "garden of forking paths" leading up to the servant's death but which path he takes is still up to him. No matter the path, the servant eventually dies. His death is unavoidable *no matter what the servant does*. Usually when we think of fatalism, we think of it along the lines of local fatalism.

Global fatalism, as well as local fatalism, can be defined more precisely in terms of *events*. **Events** are things that happen, like parties and baseball games. Events are similar to objects in that they are individuals, located at particular times (Casati and Varzi 2010). Events are opposed to **facts**, which are states of affairs that obtain. It is fact that Obama is President of the USA even though the event of his becoming president has passed. According to **global fatalism**, all events are fated; everything that happens, must happen. If events are particular, "local fatalism" cannot be defined in terms of events. It was fated that the servant was going to die but he might have died in any number of ways. There might not have been any particular fated event that was his death. **Local fatalism** is the view that some things are fated and some things are not.

If nothing is avoidable, then no one is or ever was able to do otherwise. Hence, if global fatalism is true, then so is free will skepticism, given the classical view. In the remainder of this chapter, we assume the classical view and explore other reasons for endorsing free will skepticism, threats to our freedom and control given thoughts about time, truth, foreknowledge, and determinism.[5]

1.3 Time and Truth

Some threats to free will arise given the natures of time and truth. We begin with *time*. According to **presentism**, the only things that exist are things that exist in the present (Markosian 2009; Conee and Sider 2005, Ch. 3). Consider the house that my family lived in when I was born, which existed in New Jersey but has since been replaced by a parking lot. The presentist can admit that the house did exist but he holds that it does not exist since it doesn't exist *now*.

Eternalism, on the other hand, is the view that past and future things exist as well as present things. Contrast the house noted above with the house that I lived in while in high school, which is still in New Jersey. We all recognize that the house that I lived in while in high school exists, even if it doesn't exist *here*. The eternalist merely extends this intuition about *places* to *times*. He believes, for instance, that the house that I lived in when I was born exists even though it doesn't exist now. Where or when does it exist? It exists in the *past*, according to the eternalist.

Eternalism holds that time is space-like in an *ontological* sense: time is just another dimension like one of the three spatial dimensions. Thus, many eternalists adopt **four-dimensionalism** about objects, where the universe and the things in it are regarded as four-dimensional spacetime **worms**. The world is spread throughout spacetime from the beginning of its existence until the end; individuals are four-dimensional parts of the world. The eternalist is not committed to four-dimensionalism, for one is a theory of time and the other is a theory of the identity of objects over time (Sider 2001). But at the very least four-dimensionalism is helpful in illustrating eternalism.

Some philosophers and scientists believe that if the *theory of relativity* were true, then eternalism would be true. For instance, Albert Einstein writes: "The four-dimensional mode of consideration of the 'world' is natural on the theory of relativity, since according to this theory time is robbed of its independence" (1920). Not everyone agrees with Einstein (Hinchliff 1996; Zimmerman forthcoming). Nonetheless, the four-dimensional view is a natural view to adopt, given relativity theory.

One could argue that if eternalism is true, then no one is able to do otherwise. Thus, eternalism leads to global fatalism. Consider this poetic argument from T. S. Eliot, writing with Einstein's relativity theory in mind:

> Time present and time past
> Are both perhaps present in time future,
> And time future contained in time past.
> If all time is eternally present
> All time is unredeemable.

What might have been is an abstraction
Remaining a perpetual possibility
Only in a world of speculation.
What might have been and what has been
Point to one end, which is always present.
Footfalls echo in the memory
Down the passage which we did not take
Towards the door we never opened
Into the rose-garden. My words echo
Thus, in your mind. (1935)

The passage begins with the assumption of eternalism: where objects in the past, present, and future are all equally real. According to Eliot, "what might have been is an abstraction" existing "only in a world of speculation." If eternalism is true, how is anything else possible, other than what happens? How is anyone able to do other than he in fact does? Nothing is avoidable and global fatalism is true.

Another area of intersection between time and free will is the topic of *time travel*. Consider, for instance, the *grandfather paradox* (Lewis 1976). The "grandfather paradox" refers to a family of related paradoxes that need not involve grandfathers. Some involve potential auto-infanticide, killing one's younger self (Vihvelin 1996). Others include attempts at killing one's great-great grandfather as an infant (Hawking 1996). Still others suggest the possibility of disrupting the initial meeting of one's grandparents and thus preventing a parent's birth (Deutsch and Lockwood 1994). What these examples all have in common is that they depict situations in which a time traveler is able to do something that prevents his own birth, which seems to create a paradox. How can someone who was never born prevent anything? And *who* prevented the birth?

To illustrate the grandfather paradox, I borrow a story from Lewis (1976, 75ff.). Suppose that Tim hates his grandfather so much that he wants him dead. Unfortunately for Tim, Grandfather is already dead. But Tim is no ordinary person. He has at his disposal a device that allows him to travel back in time. Suppose that Tim travels back to 1944 – a time when Grandfather was still alive but prior to the conception of either of Tim's parents. Tim aims his gun at Grandfather and attempts to shoot him. If Tim were to kill

Grandfather in 1944, then a contradiction would result. One of Tim's parents would never have been born, so Tim would never have been born. But Tim must have been born since it was he who killed Grandfather! Call this story "Tim's tale." Tim's tale has the makings of a genuine and compelling time travel paradox.

It is important to be clear on exactly what is paradoxical about Tim's tale. The argument fits the form of a *reductio ad absurdum*: we begin with the assumption that time travel is possible and deduce a contradiction from that assumption. It follows that time travel is impossible. What contradiction follows from the assumption of Tim's tale? If Tim were to kill Grandfather in 1944, then a contradiction would result: Tim would have been born (since he traveled in time to kill Grandfather) and Tim would not have been born (since Grandfather died before the birth of Tim's parents). For this reason, many people believe that backward time travel is paradoxical because if it were possible, there would be nothing to prevent contradictions. This way of formulating the grandfather paradox is faulty for at least two reasons. Most importantly, contradictions *cannot happen*, so there is no need to prevent them from being true. Logical purity is perhaps the one thing that can take care of itself.

Second, the above formulation of the grandfather paradox is incomplete. Suppose that Tim attempts to shoot Grandfather but misses. Here we have time travel without an explicit contradiction. Tim's tale, as the story is told so far, cannot lead us to conclude that time travel is impossible since no contradiction directly follows from its assumption. A contradiction only follows once we assume that Tim not only travels in time but that he kills Grandfather. There must be more to Tim's tale if we are to use it as the basis for a genuine paradox.

Let's return to the original story. Above we argued that if Tim were to kill Grandfather, then a contradiction would result. This supports the following claim:

(A)   Tim is unable to kill Grandfather.

By itself (A) is not enough to establish that time travel is impossible. What is to prevent Tim from killing Grandfather?

As Lewis says, "he has what it takes" (77). We may even suppose that at the very moment that Tim attempts to kill Grandfather another person, Tom, attempts to kill Grandfather's friend, Buddy, by shooting him with a gun (cf. Lewis 75). Tom is no time traveler, so there is little reason to suppose that he is unable to kill Buddy. Suppose that both Tim and Tom are good shots, have extensive training in firearms, are in good shape, are poised and ready to kill, have enough bullets, have made all the appropriate plans, and so on. We can add as many details to the story as we wish, enough to convince us that Tom can kill Buddy. But Tim and Tom are similar in all of the relevant respects. Consequently:

(B) Tim is able to kill Grandfather.

(A) and (B) are contradictory, and herein lies our paradox. Given the possibility of time travel, we can construct a scenario – Tim's tale – where (A) and (B) are both true. Yet (A) and (B) cannot both be true. Thus, time travel is impossible.

Both puzzles noted above – the apparent conflict between classical free will and eternalism as well as the grandfather paradox – are paradoxical but neither is necessarily problematic for free will. For one thing, we can always deny that eternalism is true or that time travel is possible. It is not so clear that this evasion works, or if it does work, that it doesn't carry with it even further consequences. For it is not clear that the real problem has to do with the nature of time as much as it does the nature of *truth*. Thankfully, some of the best solutions to the grandfather paradox, including Lewis's own contextualist response, mirror versions of compatibilism and are discussed below (§§ 3.1–2; 5.3).

An argument for global fatalism can be generated given the **tenseless view of truth** (cf. Markosian 2009):

- All propositions are true *simpliciter*, not at a time;
- All propositions are either true or false;
- No propositions change their truth-values.

Ned Markosian (2009, §1) argues that global fatalism follows from the tenseless view of truth. If it is true *now* that I'll wear my black converse sneakers tomorrow, then it is unavoidable and I cannot do otherwise. Here is a slightly altered version of his argument.

1. The tenseless view of truth is true.
2. If (1), then there exists a set of propositions that, when taken together, entail everything that was true, is true, or will be true.
3. If there exists a set of propositions that entail everything that was true, is true, or will be true, then nothing is avoidable.
4. Therefore, nothing is avoidable (and global fatalism is true).

This is a compelling argument. But is it sound?

Following John Perry (2004; cf. § 3.1), we may distinguish between a proposition's *being true* and a proposition's *being made true*. According to the tenseless view of truth, there is no **time of truth**, no particular time that a proposition becomes true. All propositions are eternally true, given the tenseless view. Propositions are *made true* by either events or worldly facts. Hence, in addition to the time of truth we can talk about the **time of event** (or the time of fact), that is, the time that the event that is the truthmaker of the proposition occurs (or the time that the fact that is the truthmaker of the proposition obtains). I raise my right hand and thereby make it the case that my right hand is raised. Given this way of thinking, a proposition is unavoidable for a person so long as he is unable to make the proposition false. Just because a proposition is true it doesn't follow that it couldn't have been *made true*. One might argue that propositions are avoidable so long as they have not been made true, together with some other conditions. Thus, (3) in Markosian's argument for global fatalism is questionable.

Of course, one might deny premise (1) and the tenseless view of truth. If one is a presentist, for instance, it might be more natural to hold the **tensed view of truth**.

- Some propositions are true at a time, not *simpliciter*;
- Some propositions are neither true nor false;
- Some propositions change their truth-values.

Certainly adopting the tensed view of truth will get one out of any problems raised by the tenseless view of truth. But the cost is a more complicated view of truth. My own view is that life is complicated and one should simplify whenever possible. This leads me to want to defend the tenseless view.

1.4 Foreknowledge

Many people think that global fatalism is true because they endorse one of several propositions about God and his nature. For the sake of discussion, suppose that God is a perfect being who has the divine attributes essentially. We need not discuss all of the divine attributes but omnipotence, benevolence, omniscience, eternality, and immutability are worth noting. One might argue that since God is the creator of everything, God must also be the cause of everything. Thus, since evil exists, God must be the cause of evil (Augustine 1993). This is a version of the **problem of evil**, which holds that the mere existence of evil, or perhaps the degree of evil in the actual world, is a puzzle given God's nature. A thorough discussion of this problem is not possible in this text but if God is the creator of everything, it is hard to see how humans can have any control over the events of the world, and thus over their actions. The claim that God is the cause of everything seems to bump up against the free will thesis. But few contemporary philosophers believe that God is the cause of *everything*, at least in the sense noted above, which seems to exclude free will.

More familiar worries arise when contemplating God's omniscience. Omniscience is *perfect knowledge*. Thus, if God is omniscient he has no contradictory beliefs and he knows every proposition that is true. There are two ways in which God could know everything that is true, depending on whether one adopts the tensed or tenseless view of truth. If God has **complete foreknowledge**, then at any time God knows everything that was true, is true, or will be true. On the other hand, the tensed view of truth may hold. According to this view, some future tensed propositions – Joe will wear his black converse sneakers tomorrow – are neither truth nor false. This proposition becomes true when I put the shoes on tomorrow, or false when and if I fail to do so. Perhaps God knows all the truths yet he only has *partial foreknowledge*.

But if God has complete foreknowledge, how can anything *be otherwise*? And if nothing can be otherwise, how is anyone able to *do* otherwise? It seems that free will is an illusion, given complete foreknowledge, especially if we adopt the classical view (see Hasker 1989; Zagzebski 2002, 2008). One line of argument goes that if God knows that I'm going to wear my black converse sneakers tomorrow, then he knew that proposition at the moment of earth's creation, or at some time before I was born at any rate. There is a time t_0 in the *remote past*, prior to the existence of human beings, when God knew that I would wear my black converse sneakers tomorrow. Yet I have no choice about the remote past. Supposing that God is immutable and changeless, I have no choice about whether God believed at t_0 that I would wear my black converse sneakers tomorrow. Thus, I have no choice about whether I wear my black converse sneakers tomorrow. The argument can be generalized and global fatalism appears to follow.

Linda Zagzebski (2002, 2008) notes at least seven potential solutions to the problem of foreknowledge and free will and we have one to add, as well.[6] Two of these – the **Frankfurtian/Augustinian Solution** as well as one dealing with issues in modal logic (the necessity of the past, the denial of the transfer of necessity principle) – are not discussed here since they are similar to results discussed later, in the sections devoted to the problem of free will and determinism (§§ 1.5, 3.1–3.2, 5.3).

Two of Zagzebski's other views are intimately related: the **open theism view** and the **Aristotelian view**. Both note that since partial foreknowledge does not entail global fatalism, if we assume that God has only partial foreknowledge and not complete foreknowledge, there is no problem for classical free will. The Aristotelian view is essentially an acceptance of the tensed view of truth, or at least a denial of the tenseless view. The open theism view focuses instead on God's lack of complete foreknowledge, explicitly rejecting the thesis of determinism and adopting a libertarian view of free will. Given our definitions of "partial foreknowledge" these views are indistinguishable. That is not to say that they are the same. But the difference is too subtle for us to appreciate.

Next is the **Boethian solution**. God might be eternal in either of two different ways (Pike 1965, 29–30). First, God might be *omnitemporal*, that is, God exists at all times. Second, God might be *atemporal*, that is, God does not exist at any time but rather exists *outside of time*. Many philosophers think that the atemporal view of eternality provides a solution to the problem of complete foreknowledge (Boethius 2001). Many others, including myself, think that such a view is incomprehensible and unhelpful. Indeed, what could one be talking about when one says that something exists outside of time? This is not to deny that it is impossible but a better, more truthful response might be to simply say, "There is a solution but I can't tell you what it is." This is a kind of **mysticism**. We touch on these issues later (§ 5.4), though in general when we cannot speak, we should remain silent.

Ockhamism distinguishes between *soft facts about the past* and *hard facts about the past*. The former are *temporally relational* whereas the latter are *temporally nonrelational*. Only **hard facts** about the past, temporally nonrelational facts, are necessarily true. According to this view, **soft facts** about the past are not actually *about the past*. Consider the claim *that yesterday it was true that Joe will wear his black converse sneakers tomorrow*. Is this proposition really about the past? *That Joe will wear his black converse sneakers tomorrow* is a proposition about the future, one that will be made true or false by events that take place tomorrow, not events that took place yesterday. This proposition – *that Joe will wear his black converse sneakers tomorrow* – would be a hard fact were it a fact about the past but as it stands it is a fact about the future (if it is a fact). For this reason, our main proposition – *that yesterday it was true that Joe will wear his black converse sneakers tomorrow* – is a soft fact about the past. It isn't really about the past; it is about the future. Similarly, *that God knows that Joe will wear his black converse sneakers tomorrow* is a soft fact about the past, so the proposition is not necessarily true.

John Martin Fischer has an interesting reply. He writes: "it is very important to distinguish two sets of issues: first, temporal nonrelationality and relationality (e.g. hardness and softness), and second, fixity and non-fixity (e.g. being out of one's control and being in one's control). I shall argue that God's prior beliefs are in the class of soft facts that are nevertheless fixed" (1994, 115). In other words, even if propositions about the past are not hard facts about the past, it might still follow that complete foreknowledge poses a problem for free will. There might be, as Fischer (117) puts it, "hard-type soft facts" that undermine our freedom and control just as much as hard facts.

According to **Molinism**, God's foreknowledge is deduced from his knowledge of the past together with various *counterfactuals of freedom*. **Counterfactuals of freedom** are conditionals like:

- If Joe were to wear his biking shorts, then he would wear his black converse sneakers.
- If Joe were to wear his dress shorts, then he would wear his brown sandals.

This is an oversimplification of the view since the counterfactuals might be more complex than either of these examples suggest. Also, there would be more counterfactuals of freedom at God's disposal, even in a given situation, than the two mentioned above. One might understand the view better if one considered the possibility of an infinite set of propositions along these lines:

- If Joe were to ride his bike to work while it was raining on a day that he was teaching, then he would wear his black converse sneakers.

Hopefully, you get the picture. One might even argue that counterfactuals of freedom ensure that the agent is able to do otherwise, for they ground the relevant powers and abilities (cf. *dispositionalism*, § 5.3). Nonetheless, God is able to predict, knowing the counterfactuals together with other facts about the past and present, the future in complete detail. Or so the story goes.

In regard to counterfactuals of freedom, William Hasker asks: "Who or what is it (if anything) that *brings it about* that these propositions are true?" (1989, 39) One might argue that it can't be the agent, for counterfactuals of freedom are eternally true (given the tenseless view of truth). They are part of the data that God uses to determine how the world goes. But if counterfactuals of freedom are not up to agents, then they start to look like laws of nature, generalizations that can be used to predict a person's behavior yet over which the person seems to have no control. The problem of free will and foreknowledge starts to look a lot like the problem of free will and determinism (§ 1.5). Given Molinism, complete foreknowledge is as problematic as the thesis of determinism. This is only a relative critique but since the consensus view is that complete foreknowledge is less problematic for free will than is determinism, it is worth noting.

Where does this leave us? One can make a reasonable case that at least some counterfactuals of freedom are true *because* of the free actions of human agents. That is, some human actions are *truthmakers* for counterfactuals of freedom, or perhaps the *consequences* of some of our actions are truthmakers for counterfactuals of freedom. In high school, for instance, I was a wrestler and in my senior year I was quite good, MVP of my high school wrestling team. It is at least plausible to suppose that, through extensive training, I eventually made the following counterfactual true:

- If someone were to attempt a cradle on me during a wrestling match, then I would counter that move with a sit-out.

Cradles and sit-outs are two of the kinds of acts that a wrestler might perform. Perhaps another example would be better.

Suppose that when he was a young man Johnson was prone to shouting fits in certain situations, G′. Suppose, further, that Johnson underwent extensive therapy and that eventually he overcame his outbursts of anger. Instead of throwing a fit, he taught himself to count to ten in situation G′ and that in this way he was able to contain his rage. Let G* be those situations in Johnson's life that occur after his recovery that are similar to situation G′. At this later point in his life it seems that Johnson, through his own free actions, made the following counterfactual true:

- If G* were to obtain, then Johnson would count to ten.

There are numerous examples like these in which people train – or retrain – themselves to perform certain actions in a certain situation, or to act differently than they have acted in past situations that were similar. It is dubious to suggest that no counterfactuals of freedom are made true by the efforts of human beings.

Worries about foreknowledge can be generated without presuming that God exists. Consider the *Matrix* trilogy. When the Oracle first meets Neo she already knows a lot about him (*The Matrix*, Ch. 22). The Oracle knows that Neo will break a vase before he breaks it. She knows that Trinity likes Neo and that Neo needs to make an important choice between saving Morpheus and saving himself. She even knows that Neo is the One. Neo's aversion to being the One, as the Oracle reveals, comes from his belief that he is in control. He refuses to acknowledge that he is the One partly because he knows that the One is in the grips of fate yet Neo thinks that having his future all planned out compromises his freedom.

In *Matrix Reloaded* (Ch. 13), after the Oracle offers Neo a piece of candy, they have the following dialogue.

NEO: You already know if I'm going to take it.
ORACLE: I wouldn't be much of an oracle if I didn't.
NEO: But if you already know, how can I make a choice?

The *Matrix* trilogy seeks not just to raise the problem of foreknowledge and free will but to solve it. Foreknowledge does not destroy free will, for the prophesies about Neo are true *and* Neo is in complete control. Much of this book is devoted to exploring a similar response to the problem of free will and determinism.

The problems discussed so far are profound but they don't worry most contemporary philosophers too much. The big worry, among contemporary philosophers, comes from the threat of *determinism*. Determinism is more worrisome than time, or truth, or foreknowledge because the threat to free will remains even if we deny determinism! The **problem of free will** is really two problems: the problem of free will and determinism together with the *problem of luck*, or the problem of free will and indeterminism (van Inwagen 2008; Strawson

1986, 2002, 2004). This problem is so difficult and so basic that if we solve it, likely we can solve the others, as well.

It is worth highlighting that threats to free will have a variety of sources and can be generated from a variety of distinct worldviews. One might adopt a religious worldview and feel the threat due to God's foreknowledge or God's preordination or God's immutability. Or one might adopt a scientific worldview and feel the threat from eternalism or from natural, causal explanations of the world around us. As we shall see, even if determinism is false, there might still be a threat to free will since on that picture our actions appear to be random, uncaused events (§§ 1.5, 3.3). Worries about free will are inescapable regardless of one's view of the world.

1.5 Determinism

Informally, *determinism* is the thesis that "given the past and the laws of nature, there is only one possible future" (van Inwagen 1983, 65). Determinism is usually understood as a *causal thesis*: past events together with the laws of nature bring about future events. But we should be careful to distinguish determinism from the thesis of **universal causality**: every event has a cause. Perhaps quantum mechanics requires indeterminism but it doesn't follow from this that quantum events are uncaused. Quantum laws might be probabilistic, so there can be universal causality without determinism.

The cause–effect relation is a relation between events. You strike a match and it ignites. The striking and the ignition are two separate events, the first one causing the second. *Actions* are things that happen, too, so they are kinds of events. Laws of nature are propositions, not events. **Propositions** are the ultimate bearers of truth-value. Events occur or do not occur but propositions are either true or false. The striking of the match is something that happens, not something that is true or false. *That the match is struck* is true or false and it is a proposition. There is a link between propositions and events: an event occurs if and only if the *corresponding proposition* – i.e. *that* the event occurs – is true. Perhaps, there is a similar link between events and facts.

The standard definition of "determinism" is given in terms of *entailment*, which is a relation between propositions. **Determinism** is true if and only if a complete description of any past state of the universe together with the laws of nature entails each and every true proposition.[7] This is related to the **Laplacean definition of "determinism,"** according to which:

> We ought to regard the present state of the universe as the effect of its antecedent state and as the cause of the state that is to follow. An intelligence knowing all the forces acting in nature at a given instant, as well as the momentary positions of all things in the universe, would be able to comprehend in one single formula the motions of the largest bodies as well as the lightest atoms in the world, provided that its intellect were sufficiently powerful to subject all data to analysis; to it nothing would be uncertain, the future as well as the past would be present to its eyes. The perfection that the human mind has been able to give to astronomy affords but a feeble outline of such an intelligence. (Laplace, in Hoefer 2010)

We should distinguish between *determinism* and the thesis of **universal predictability**, according to which every event is predictable. Laplace is famous for defining determinism in terms of the ability of a divine being to make predictions. Yet it turns out that some deterministic worlds are *chaotic*, and thus unpredictable (Hoefer 2010).

In *Waking Life* (Richard Linklater 2001), David Sosa discusses the problem of free will with Main Character. Perhaps the world operates in accordance with the fundamental laws of physics, which govern the behavior of all things. If each of us is a physical system, then our behavior is subject to these same laws.[8] This is the problem of free will and determinism: if determinism is true, then no one has free will. Or so it seems. We might think that our chances for free will improve if indeterminism is true but Sosa suggests that if the world is indeterministic – if everything is the result of the unpredictable behavior of small quantum particles, for instance – that won't help either. For on that hypothesis our acts are nothing more than random swerves in a chaotic system. If that is so, how can anything be up to us? There is not much room for free will on either model, whether determinism is true or not.

The discussion between Sosa and Main Character reveals the two sides of the problem of free will: the problem of free will and determinism plus the problem of luck. According to the **problem of luck**, indeterminism introduces randomness and that is counter to our actions being up to us. Thus, even if it is not the case that our acts are determined, there might still be a problem for free will. If we put these two problems together – the problem of free will and determinism and the problem of luck – we get the problem of free will (van Inwagen 2004, 2008). It is best illustrated by the **free will dilemma**:

1. If determinism is true, then no one has free will.
2. If indeterminism is true, then no one has free will.
3. Therefore, no one has free will.

Since free will is deemed by most philosophers to be necessary for moral responsibility, free will skepticism often leads to **skepticism about moral responsibility**, the view that no one is morally responsible for anything. Thus, the problem of free will has consequences that, if not worrisome, are at least offensive to common sense as well as contrary to the basic tenets of several religious and moral theories. This problem (Chs 3 and 4) and various solutions (Ch. 5) are discussed in detail later in this book. In the remainder of this chapter, we explain the free will dilemma in more detail and introduce some useful terminology.

Premise (1) of the free will dilemma is the claim of *incompatibilism*. According to *compatibilism*, the free will thesis is consistent with determinism. Compatibilism is not merely the claim that some events (e.g. actions) are free and some events are determined. This is consistent with indeterminism. Rather, **compatibilism** is the stronger thesis that the very same act may be both free and fully determined. **Incompatibilism** is the denial of compatibilism.

Compatibilism, incompatibilism, and free will skepticism come in various forms (James 1956; van Inwagen 1983). **Hard determinists** are incompatibilists who endorse determinism but deny the free will thesis, so they are also free will skeptics. **Libertarians** are incompatibilists who deny determinism and endorse the free will thesis. **Soft determinists** are compatibilists who accept both determinism and the free will thesis. Developments in physics, specifically in quantum mechanics, have led many to reject determinism, so examples of soft and hard determinism are rare though not impossible.[9] A better classification of the three main contemporary views is *libertarianism*, *compatibilism*, and *free will skepticism* (cf. Campbell, O'Rourke, and Shier 2004b, 3–7). These three theories are discussed in the remainder of the book; little more is said about soft determinism or hard determinism.

Why accept incompatibilism and premise (1)? Determinism is a *conditional* thesis: *given* the past and laws, there is only one future. How do we get from this conditional thesis to free will skepticism? For many philosophers, **the consequence argument** provides the answer.

> If determinism is true, then our acts are the consequences of the laws of nature and events in the remote past. But it is not up to us what went on before we were born, and neither is it up to us what the laws of nature are. Therefore, the consequences of these things are not up to us. (van Inwagen 1983, 16)

The first premise of the consequence argument follows from the definition of "determinism." The second premise is more interesting, for according to it the past and the laws are not up to us. What does this mean, given the classical view?

Intuitively, there are a great number of propositions about the world that are up to us in the sense that we might *render* each either true or false (van Inwagen 1983, 66–7; § 2.1). I am able to raise my hand, thereby rendering it true that my hand is raised. Or I can leave my hand where it is, thereby rendering it false that my hand is raised. This is one way of thinking about my power over the world around me. The second premise of the consequence argument claims that this power is not absolute. Among the propositions that I am unable to render false are the laws of nature and true propositions about the past. I am unable to render the law of gravity false. Nor am I able to render it false that Barack Obama was elected president of the USA in 2008 (Lewis 1981; van Inwagen 1983; Perry 2004). This all seems to support premise (1) of the free will dilemma, given the classical view.

What follows, according to the consequence argument, is that, given determinism, no one is able to render any true proposition false. Thus, no one is ever able to do otherwise and the free will thesis is false, given the classical view. The actions that I perform are just the ones that follow necessarily from the past and the laws of nature. Since, at any time, I have no choice about the past and the laws, it follows that I have no choice about my action. Free will skepticism follows from determinism, according to the consequence argument. The consequence argument is discussed in more detail below (§§ 3.1–2).

Determinism is not the only problem for free will; *in*determinism is equally problematic. Here is van Inwagen's example of **the problem of luck** supporting premise (2):

> . . . does postulating or asserting that the laws of nature are indeterministic provide any comfort to those who would like to believe in [classical free will]? If the laws are indeterministic, then more than one future is indeed consistent with those laws and the actual past and present – but how can anyone have any choice about which of these futures becomes actual? Isn't it a matter of chance which becomes actual? If God were to "return" an indeterministic world to precisely its state at some time in the past, and then let the world go forward again, things might indeed happen differently the "second" time. But then, if the world is indeterministic, isn't it just a matter of chance how things did happen in the one, actual course of events? And if what we do is just a matter of chance – well, who would want to call that freedom? (van Inwagen 1998, 370)

Whether one adopts the classical view or the source view, how can indeterminism help? Wherever there is indeterminism, there is chance and luck and neither can contribute to an agent's free will. Neither can "increase or procure" (Balaguer 2010, 119) the agent's free will.

There is a related story to the one above illustrating the compatibility problem. Suppose that God "returns" the world to the same state 100 times over and each time things turn out the same. Our acts would be compulsive rather than free. The two stories can be combined. Suppose you make a choice between two alternatives 100 times over and each time the choice is the same. Compulsion. Suppose now you split the choice, half the time choosing one option, half the time the other. Luck. How can a combination of the two make things better? This is the problem of free will.

Perhaps a better dilemma than the free will dilemma is the **indeterminism-can't-help argument**.

1.   If determinism is true, then no one has free will.
2'.   Indeterminism can't help.
3.   Therefore, no one has free will.

Galen Strawson is a proponent of such arguments for free will skepticism (§§ 3.4, 4.3) and here are some quotes from Strawson supporting premise (2'):

○   How can our claim to moral responsibility be improved by the supposition that it is partly a matter of chance or random outcome that we and our actions are as they are? (2004, Introduction)
○   . . . it is foolish to suppose that indeterministic or random factors, for which one is *ex hypothesi* in no way responsible, can in themselves contribute to one's being truly or ultimately responsible for how one is. (2004, § 3)
○   . . . indeterministic occurrences cannot possibly contribute to moral responsibility . . . Indeterminism gives rise to unpredictability, not responsibility. It cannot help in any way at all. (2004, § 5)
○   . . . indeterministic occurrences can never be a source of true (moral) responsibility. (2004, § 6)

On this reading of the argument, considerations of luck are intended to support premise (2') of the indeterminism-can't-help argument rather than premise (2) of the free will dilemma. The problem of luck suggests that particular manifestations of indeterminism are threatening to our free will. If they are a genuine threat, it is because indeterminism introduces an element of chance into the causal chains leading up to our actions. One cannot generalize from this fact to a conclusion that supports premise (2) of the free will dilemma, for the mere truth of indeterminism does not entail that our actions are undetermined. (2') is only significant if we already have a problem with determinism, that is, if we already have reason to believe in incompatibilism: premise (1) of both arguments. For this reason, I think that something like the indeterminism-can't-help argument is underlying many of the arguments for free will skepticism and its soundness rests on the thesis of incompatibilism, for determinism is deemed a threat to freedom and indeterminism is only problematic because it cannot help.

Van Inwagen admits as much about the *Mind* argument. Suppose that indeterminism is true but that the only instance of causal indeterminism occurs in some far away region of spacetime, outside the light cone of any local event. How do van Inwagen's observations about indeterministic luck show that local agents lack free will? They don't and they can't, as van Inwagen knows. He writes:

> Incompatibilists maintain that free will requires indeterminism. But it should be clear even to them that not just any sort of indeterminism will do. Suppose, for example, that there is exactly one undetermined particle of matter somewhere in the universe, and that it is far from any rational agent, the rest of the universe being governed entirely by strict, deterministic laws. In that case, determinism is, strictly speaking, false. But, clearly, if determinism is incompatible with free will, so is the thesis that everything except one distant particle of matter is determined. (1983, 126)

The main point here can be generalized to cover any argument given in support of (3). Determinism entails that every act is determined by prior causes. Indeterminism does not entail anything about the causal structure of the world leading up to any particular human action. Thus, indeterminism cannot entail that every act is undetermined let alone that every act is a matter of luck. The *Mind* argument cannot support premise (3).

Reflections along these lines reveal that the free will dilemma might not be the best argument for free will skepticism. A better argument might be the indeterminism-can't-help argument. But rather than get caught up in these debates, we'll stick with the free will dilemma. In Chapter 2, we locate the problem of free will within the broader subject of the metaphysics of moral responsibility. After that we investigate a spectrum of arguments: some argue for incompatibilism (§§ 3.1–3.3) or **incompatibilism about moral responsibility** (§§ 4.1–4.2) – roughly, the incompatibility between moral responsibility and determinism – while others argue more directly for either free will skepticism (§ 3.4) or skepticism about moral responsibility (§ 4.3). We close with a discussion of a spectrum of theories of free will (Ch. 5).

Further Reading

Kane (2005) provides an excellent introduction to free will that contrasts nicely with this book. Schick (2002) and McKenna (2005) provide introductory discussions of the issues of free will, fatalism, and foreknowledge in relation to the *Matrix* trilogy. Taylor (1963, 1992) and Markosian (2009) offer compelling versions of arguments for global fatalism that make no presuppositions about determinism or foreknowledge. For more on problems about divine foreknowledge, see Kretzmann (1966), Hasker (1989), Kane (2005, Ch. 13), and Zagzebski (2008).

Pereboom (1997) and Kane (2002a) are two valuable and affordable collections of essays. Kane (2002b) and Campbell, O'Rourke, and Shier (2004) are recommended for the more advanced readers. Many of the definitions and arguments given in this book originate in van Inwagen (1983).

Films about Free Will

- *The Matrix* (Andy and Larry Wachowski, 1999)
- *The Matrix: Reloaded* (Andy and Larry Wachowski, 2003)
- *Waking Life* (Richard Linklater, 2001)
- *Stranger Than Fiction* (Marc Forster, 2006)
- *Groundhog Day* (Harold Ramis, 1993)
- *Sliding Doors* (Peter Howitt, 1998)
- *Run Lola Run* (Tom Tykwer, 1998)
- *The Butterfly Effect* (Eric Bress, 2004)
- *Twelve Monkeys* (Terry Gilliam, 1995)

2
Moral Responsibility

Metaphysics is the study of the ultimate nature of reality, that is, the study of reality in its most general characteristics. In the **metaphysics of moral responsibility**, we examine questions about the fundamental nature of moral responsibility. What is moral responsibility? Does moral responsibility require free will? Is it possible for an agent to be morally responsible for anything if determinism is true? What other necessary conditions must obtain in order for an agent to be morally responsible for something? Is anyone morally responsible for anything?

The hope of this chapter is that we might better understand the concept of *free will* by taking a step backwards and seeing how it plays a role in the broader *metaphysics of moral responsibility*. Two central questions are investigated: what is moral responsibility (§ 2.1) and what conditions are necessary for it (§§ 2.2–2.3)? As we've noted, there are two main views of freedom: free will as the ability to do otherwise and freedom as sourcehood. Later in the chapter, we discuss the "free will" crisis, e.g. the worry about *monism* (§ 1.2), that there is no single, univocal usage of the term "free will" (§ 2.4). We offer our provisional understanding – free will is the power of up-to-usness – as a solution to the "free will" crisis. We close by considering the possibility of a theory of moral responsibility without free will (§ 2.5).

2.1   Moral Responsibility

For what *kinds* of things are persons morally responsible (van Inwagen 2004, 220)? We influence the world directly through our *actions* and indirectly through the **consequences** of our actions. Actions are kinds of *events*, things that happen. Since actions are events, the consequences of our actions can be understood as other events caused by our actions: Jason flips the switch and the room is illuminated. The flipping of the switch causes the lamp to light and this, in turn, illuminates the room. Donald Davidson (1963) notes that action ascriptions have an *accordion effect*: Jason moves his finger, Jason flips the switch, Jason lights the lamp, Jason alerts the burglar, Jason thwarts the crime. All may be viable descriptions of the same action. The line between action and consequence becomes blurred when we think of the consequences of our actions as other events caused by our actions. We might take the consequences of our actions to be proposition-like *facts*, state of affairs that obtain (van Inwagen 2004, 220ff.). Since it is a lot easier to talk about moral responsibility for *actions*, and given the accordion effect and the fact that one can move easily from events to facts, we speak of responsibility about actions.

Given that we are responsible for our actions, what *is* moral responsibility? Consider two possible interpretations of P. F. Strawson's (1962) theory of moral responsibility, the details of which are discussed later in this book (§ 5.4). First, there is the **constitutive account**. According to this view, one is morally responsible for an action if and only if one is actually praised or blamed for the action by members of one's moral community (Watson 1987b, 257; Fischer and Ravizza 1993b, 16). The phrase "one's moral community" is intentionally vague. You get different versions of the constitutive account depending on which individuals are selected and how those classes are determined. The main point is that according to this account, reactive attitudes like praise and blame are *constitutive* of moral responsibility. To say that the reactive attitudes are constitutive of moral responsibility is to say that the attitudes of praise and blame themselves are essential to whether a person is morally responsible. According to this view, if no one is ever praised or blamed, then no one is morally responsible for anything.

The constitutive account is open to a clear and decisive criticism, for as John Martin Fischer and Mark Ravizza note, there is a "difference between being *held* responsible and actually *being* responsible" (1993b, 18). Consider Roger O. Thornhill, the Cary Grant character in Alfred Hitchcock's film, *North by Northwest* (1959). Thornhill is universally blamed as a murderer by the members of his moral community yet he is an innocent man. In short, it does not follow from the fact that one is blamed for an action that he is indeed blameworthy, regardless of who does the blaming. Often the praiseworthy go unnoticed and the blameworthy get off scot-free. Given this, we adopt the **standard account**: one is morally responsible for an action only if the act is praiseworthy or blameworthy.

2.2 Freedom and Epistemic Conditions

What conditions are necessary for moral responsibility? Aristotle noted two kinds of conditions: *freedom conditions* and *epistemic conditions* (Aristotle 1985, 1ff.; cf. Fischer and Ravizza 1993b and 1998, 12ff.). Each is discussed in this section in turn.

We should avoid looking for *the* freedom condition that is necessary for moral responsibility. As Al Mele notes, there are likely stronger and weaker kinds of freedom, all of which are necessary for moral responsibility. If we are going to be monists (§ 1.2), we should talk about *the strongest freedom*, the freedom that is most fundamental to moral responsibility (Mele 2006, 27, fn. 18). A pluralist might hold that there are various kinds of freedom, each one of which is relevant to moral responsibility (Balaguer 2010). This all speaks against our propensity to seek *the* freedom that is necessary for moral responsibility. Maybe there is no single freedom that is up to the task.

Not everyone uses "free will" to designate the most fundamental freedom condition for moral responsibility. **Semicompatibilism** is the view that even though some freedoms – for instance, the ability to do otherwise – are incompatible with determinism, moral responsibility is compatible with determinism. A semicompatibilist might be a classical theorist and think that free will (the ability to do otherwise) is incompatible with determinism but that moral responsibility is compatible with determinism, since moral responsibility does not require the ability to do otherwise (Fischer 1994, § 5.3).

Nearly everyone believes that some kind of freedom or control is necessary for moral responsibility. We don't want to get caught-up in pointless linguistic debates, like whether free will or some *other* freedom is *the* kind of freedom we're after (Balaguer 2010). Whether we happen to call it "free will" or not can't matter. Nor do we want to make the connection between free will and moral responsibility a matter of stipulation (van Inwagen 2008). On the other hand, the term "free will" has a technical, historical use as well as a common sense understanding. It is hard to see how we are not all talking about the same thing but it is difficult to agree about what that thing is. This is a contentious issue among contemporary philosophers.

Aristotle's freedom condition is that the origin of the actions must be in the agent. When "the origin of the actions is in" the agent, "it is also up to him to do them or not to do them" (Aristotle 1985, 2). We need not worry now about what it means for the origin of the actions to be *in* the agent, for Aristotle links it to the power of up-to-usness.

Any adequate freedom condition for moral responsibility is going to require a *tracing* component (Vargas 2005). Consider this example:

> DRUNK DRIVER Smith begins drinking at 7 pm and a few hours later he gets in his car and drives home down a dark road in the middle of the night. At 11 pm he is driving well over the speed limit and he is so drunk that both his vision and his reaction time are greatly impaired. A moment later, at 11:01 pm, he strikes and kills Jones who is walking in a crosswalk. (Campbell 2005; cf. van Inwagen 1989, 236, and Mele 2006, 84–5)

Suppose that the classical view of free will is correct. Since Smith was unable at 11:01 pm to do otherwise, one might argue that he was unable to avoid killing the pedestrian and not morally responsible for doing so. Nonetheless, Smith was able at 7 pm to avoid drinking. He was able at some earlier time to avoid driving. He was able at some later time to avoid speeding. This provides some evidence for the **classical freedom (with tracing) condition**: a person is morally responsible for an act only if he is or was able to do otherwise. There is a related *source freedom (with tracing) condition* (cf. Kane 1996). Combining the above insights, we get our **freedom (with tracing) condition**: a person is morally responsible for an act only if the act is or was up to him.

In addition to a freedom condition, philosophers generally agree with Aristotle that there is an epistemic condition for moral responsibility. Here is the **first approximate** epistemic condition:

- a person is morally responsible for an action only if he has knowledge about the particulars of that action.

This principle suggests, for instance, that the agent should know that he is performing the action, what he is doing, for what purpose he is doing it, how he is doing it, and what instrument he is using. These are just some of the considerations that Aristotle notes. Ignorance of any of these types of knowledge generally constitutes a mitigating factor, one that lessens the agent's praiseworthiness or blameworthiness. Suppose that Gary sits in a chair that happens to be rigged to a bomb planted in another building. Gary has no idea that the chair is rigged to the bomb nor should he have known this. Nonetheless, Gary sits in the chair and innocent people die. It seems that Gary is not morally responsible for the death of innocent people, for he had no reason to suspect that by sitting in the chair he would cause a bomb to explode. Perhaps he is *causally responsible* for this event but causal responsibility is not sufficient for moral responsibility. Given this example, an epistemic condition for moral responsibility is essential. But which condition, or even what kind of condition, should we adopt?

The first approximate is also flawed since genuine *knowledge* of the particulars need not be required for moral responsibility (Ginet 2000, 269). Suppose that Gary over-hears a plot to blow up a building involving the very chair in which he wants to sit. He believes, and has good reason to believe, that the chair is connected to a bomb and that a building will blow up if he sits in the chair. Gary is an epistemic skeptic. He argues that since he knows nothing he is not morally responsible for sitting in the chair. If this argument is sound, it can be generalized.

Gary lacks knowledge yet he might be morally responsible for sitting in the chair. Moral responsibility requires *rational belief* but not genuine knowledge. It is better to express epistemic principles about moral responsibility in terms of a lack of *ignorance* on the part of the agent. This gives us a **second approximate** epistemic condition:

- a person is morally responsible for his act only if he is not ignorant about the particulars of the act (Aristotle 1985, 3–4).

Is this a sound principle about the epistemic condition of moral responsibility?

It would be nice if moral responsibility did not require genuine *knowledge*. If knowledge were required, then *epistemological skepticism* – the view that no one knows anything – would undermine moral responsibility. That is a heavy price to pay. Is there an easy response to the skeptic about knowledge? Are we sure that we *know* anything? Socrates famously argued that no one is blameworthy for anything. Wrong actions are done only out of ignorance, especially ignorance of the good. The thief believes that by stealing from his friend he is benefiting himself. If he knew that his friendship was more important than the money, he would have acted differently.

What is striking about Socrates's argument is that he argues from epistemological skepticism to skepticism about moral responsibility without saying anything about knowledge of the particulars. Moral decision-making requires complex cognitive capacities and an understanding of basic moral principles. If it turns out that no one has knowledge of moral principles, then perhaps skepticism about moral responsibility is true, too (Rosen 2004).

There is a difference, though, between Aristotle's epistemic condition, which we adopt, and the conditions noted above. The latter principles involve ignorance about moral principles whereas the former concerns ignorance about the *particulars* of action: whether the agent is performing it, what he is doing, for what purpose, and to whom? One can have rational beliefs about the particulars of his action without having knowledge of moral principles. The skeptical argument above is interesting but it is unrelated to the kinds of epistemic principles that Aristotle raises.

Michael J. Zimmerman has persuasively argued for the following **epistemic tracing principle**: "one is culpable for behaving ignorantly only if one is culpable for being ignorant" (1997, 423). A student cannot plead ignorance in an effort to avoid blame for failing an exam, for it is the student's responsibility to learn the material. Likewise, ignorance of the law is not always an excuse. We are required to know the law in most situations. Combining this with results from above gives us the **epistemic (with tracing) condition**: a person is morally responsible for his act only if he either lacked or lacks ignorance about the particulars of the act OR he was or is culpable for being ignorant.

2.3 Other Necessary Conditions

We have noted some freedom and epistemic conditions that are necessary for moral responsibility. For some philosophers, the metaphysics of moral responsibility seems to stop here. In this section we discuss other necessary conditions for moral responsibility. Some of these principles are controversial but others are generally regarded as true even if they are not always noted. In bringing them to our attention, we are in no way questioning their warrant. In fact, we regard some of these as principles of common sense, and without need of rational support. But that is another matter (§ 5.4).

To begin, there is a **moral condition** for moral responsibility: a person is morally responsible for an act only if the act is or was morally right or morally wrong. How can I be blameworthy for stealing unless stealing is wrong? This is an *external constraint* on moral responsibility similar to the truth constraint on knowledge: one knows that a proposition is true only if it is true. No one doubts this condition in discussions of the metaphysics of moral responsibility. Sometimes these considerations are folded into one's account of moral responsibility (Campbell 2005).

Cases of omission limit us from offering a more general rule. In cases of **commission**, one *commits* or *performs* an act. In cases of **omission**, an event occurs because one *fails* to prevent it from occurring. The child died because Sally failed to save him – even though Sally is a champion swimmer and was lounging by the side of the pool watching the horrible event unfold.

We might restrict moral responsibility in cases of omission with the aid of **PPA** (the principle of possible action): "A person is morally responsible for failing to perform a given act only if he could have performed that act" (van Inwagen 1978). Van Inwagen gives an example of someone who fails to make a phone call in an effort to save another's life yet, as it turns out, her telephone wire was cut and she was unable to make the call anyway. According to PPA, the person was not blameworthy for failing to call the police since she was unable to do so.

The corresponding commission condition – *the principle of alternative possibilities*, or **PAP** – is very controversial: "A person is morally responsible for what he has done only if he could have done otherwise" (Frankfurt 1969). PAP is accepted by proponents of the classical view of free will but rejected by source theorists. Notice that this is a variation of the classical freedom (with tracing) condition. We discuss this debate in more detail in the next section (§ 2.4). Given the contentious nature of PAP, van Inwagen offers additional principles in their place (van Inwagen 1978, 2004). It is worth noting that proponents of Frankfurt cases dismiss van Inwagen's new principles, for either they are equally susceptible to counterexample or they "have nothing to do with the relationship between moral responsibility and free will" (Frankfurt 1982, 294).

Many of the principles noted above entail additional **agency and continuity conditions** for moral responsibility. The pronoun "he" in PAP, for instance, suggests that the person being held responsible is *the same person as* the one who was able to do otherwise. Similarly, we tend to think that the person we blame or punish is the same person as the one who performed the wrong action. Some philosophers disagree about the literal truth of claims about personal identity like these, so perhaps it is best to understand this as a *continuity condition*, not an *identity* condition.[1] At the very least, there must be continuity between the one who could have done otherwise and the agent who performed the action, or the agent who did the deed and the one who is blameworthy for it.

Recall the previous discussion about eternalism and four-dimensionalism (§ 1.3). Eternalism holds that past and future objects exist just as much as present objects. It is natural, on this view, to think of a person as a four-dimensional *space-time worm*. Each person is a four-dimensional object extended from his birth until his death. One might argue: "I didn't rob the store. It was a three-dimensional time-slice of a spacetime worm. I'm a three-dimensional time-slice of the same space-time worm, so the two of us look the same – we have **qualitative sameness** – but we are not **numerically identical** (Conee and Sider 2005, Ch. 1). Thus, I'm not the guy who robbed the store."

Worries about personal identity need not concern us too much. According to Derek Parfit (1971), identity is not important. What is important is *psychological continuity*: that persons have the same memory, character traits, and so on. Parfit's view is distinguished from the *psychological continuity view*, held by Locke (1690), according to which persons are numerically identical if and only if they have the same "memories, character traits, etc." (Conee and Sider 2005, 15). In a sense, Parfit is not giving a theory of personal identity. He is saying that personal identity differs from psychological continuity and that psychological continuity matters, not personal identity.

Our condition is even broader since we don't require *psychological* continuity, just *continuity*. One could adopt the spatiotemporal theory and still satisfy this condition. According to the **spatiotemporal theory**, "persons are numerically identical if and only if they are spatiotemporally continuous via a series of *persons*" (Conee and Sider 2005, 13). Spatiotemporal continuity is a way of describing persons as physical beings. Some kind of continuity is essential but we remain moot about whether it should be psychological continuity or spatiotemporal continuity.

Agency and continuity conditions for moral responsibility include *agency conditions* as well as continuity conditions. Even if PAP is false and the ability to do otherwise is not required for moral responsibility, in cases of commission, we must have done *something* in order to be praiseworthy or blameworthy for anything. Moral responsibility requires agency. For instance, if Gary is blameworthy for the bank robbery, then he must have robbed the bank or planned to rob it or was somehow connected to the robbing of the bank by virtue of something that he did. His blameworthiness requires that *he* performed some bad action.

Lastly, there are **capacity conditions**. For instance, an agent is morally responsible for his actions only if he has a range of *cognitive capacities*. When my son, Lake, was two years old he was not blameworthy for his actions but at eleven years old he is. What accounts for the difference? Lake performed actions at the age of two but he had less control over his actions then than he does now. At the age of two, he didn't seem to have the kind of control required of a morally responsible agent. Some of this difference in freedom and control may be attributed to the *freedom condition* discussed above. But a great deal of the difference between Lake then and Lake now is simply due to an increase in his cognitive capacities. Much of this is easy to explain. For instance, Lake's frontal lobes are more fully developed than they were.

Development of frontal lobes corresponds directly to what R. Jay Wallace calls one's powers of "reflective self-control" (Wallace 1994, 2). Included here are "the power to grasp and apply moral reasons, and the power to control one's behavior by the light of such reasons" (7) as well as "the further powers to step back from one's desires, to reflect on the ends that they incline one to pursue in light of moral principles, and to adjust or revise one's ends as a result of such reflection" (14). According to Wallace, these powers are *skills*, "forms of broadly psychological competence or capacity, such as the general ability to speak a language, or to read musical notation and reproduce the music read on an instrument" (186).

We previously noted a debate between **fundamentalists**, philosophers who identify free will with a single fundamental power like the ability to do otherwise, and *nonfundamentalists*, who think that free will is a collection of powers (§ 1.2). Given the above, one might think that free will is the set of powers of reflective self-control or "practical reasoning" (Vihvelin 2004). Some questions emerge. Are these collective powers *skills*, as Wallace suggests? Related to this, are they dispositional powers?

According to **dispositionalism**, not only is free will a set of powers but those powers are dispositional powers. Dispositionalists might or might not agree with Wallace that the relevant powers are *skills*. Perhaps one retains the skill to speak French when he has laryngitis even though he loses the power or ability to speak.[2] Dispositions are consistent with determinism, so dispositionalism provides an interesting classical compatibilist theory of free will (Vihvelin 2004; see § 5.3).

Not everyone is convinced. Van Inwagen, for instance, offers the following criticism of dispositionalism:

> The concept of a causal power or capacity would seem to be the concept of an invariable disposition to react to certain determinate changes in the environment in certain determinate ways, whereas the concept of an agent's power to act would seem not to be the concept of a power that is dispositional or reactive, but rather the concept of a power to *originate* changes in the environment. (1983, 11)

Van Inwagen suggests that the *power to act* cannot be a dispositional power. It is an *active power* not merely a passive one.

Van Inwagen's criticism of dispositionalism is compelling. Several distinct views are worth noting. First, one might hold that free will is a fundamental active power and that the power to act includes the power to act otherwise. That is, one cannot have the former without having the latter. This is a **classical fundamentalist view**. There are **classical nonfundamentalist views**, as well. Perhaps free will is a collection of active powers and cognitive capacities (Campbell 1997). Perhaps active powers are just complex dispositional powers, too. Van Inwagen wants to deny this but isn't he just begging the question? This is one of those matters about which I am truly perplexed. Part of me is nonfundamentalist and advocates a naturalist theory of free will as a set of dispositional powers. Part of me rejects this in favor of a more fundamental freedom, one that is too rich for dispositional analysis.

Here is a short list of some of the more important conditions considered in this section. Two types of relatively uncontroversial conditions are:

- **Agency and continuity conditions**
- **Capacity conditions**

In addition, there are more detailed principles.

- **Moral condition**: a person is morally responsible for an act only if the act is or was morally right or morally wrong.
- **Freedom (with tracing) condition**: a person is morally responsible for an act only if the act is or was up to him.
- **Epistemic (with tracing) condition**: a person is morally responsible for his act only if he either lacked or lacks ignorance about the particulars of the act OR he was or is culpable for being ignorant.

Lastly, two controversial necessary conditions are worth noting.

- **PAP**: "A person is morally responsible for what he has done only if he could have done otherwise" (Frankfurt 1969).
- **PPA**: "A person is morally responsible for failing to perform a given act only if he could have performed that act" (van Inwagen 1978).

The crisis surrounding these debates is discussed in the next section (§ 2.4).

What should we say about PAP? Is it true or false? There is a natural reading of PAP that is not contentious. Even van Inwagen can agree that cognitive capacities, like the powers of reflective self-control, are necessary for moral responsibility. Further, it is harmless to add that cognitive capacities are dispositional, as well. Nor is it uncommon to associate dispositional claims with conditionals. Of course, a simple conditional *analysis* of dispositions won't work (Fara 2009). Nonetheless, it is not out of the question to suggest that if one is morally responsible for doing something, then he is or was disposed to do otherwise, if only in the weak sense given the relevant cognitive capacities: he was able to do otherwise, relative to different situations. Some version of PAP is correct (cf. Campbell 1997 and 2005). Perhaps the ability to do otherwise noted in this reading is not "robust" enough to matter but that is reading more into PAP than the mere words suggest.

2.4 The "Free Will" Crisis

The "free will" crisis is best understood as a **trilemma**: each individual claim seems true yet they appear to be mutually inconsistent.

1. Free will is necessary for moral responsibility.
2. The ability to do otherwise is necessary for free will.
3. The ability to do otherwise is *not* necessary for moral responsibility.

Claim (1) gains support since philosophers generally believe that *some* kind of freedom is necessary for moral responsibility. We don't want to say that (1) is true by definition but we've already considered several reasons to accept it. Claim (2) is the classical thesis.

Claim (3) is the denial of (PAP). One who accepts both (1) and (2), can always reject it by offering the following argument:

- A person was morally responsible for an act only if he did it freely.
- A person performed an action freely only if he was able to do otherwise.
- Therefore, (PAP) A person was morally responsible for an act only if he was able to do otherwise.

The **classical view of moral responsibility** accepts the classical view of free will as well as PAP. Recall that the *classical view* of free will holds that a person has free will only if he is or was able to do otherwise. PAP claims that moral responsibility requires the ability to do otherwise.

The above argument for PAP was convincing to most philosophers until 1969, when Harry Frankfurt devised a potential counterexample.

> Suppose someone – Black, let us say – wants Jones to perform a certain action. Black is prepared to go to considerable lengths to get his way, but he prefers to avoid showing his hand unnecessarily. So he waits until Jones is about to make up his mind what to do, and he does nothing unless it is clear to him (Black is an excellent judge of such things) that Jones is going to decide to do something *other* than what he wants him to do. If it does become clear that Jones is going to decide to do something else, Black takes effective steps to ensure that Jones decides to do, and that he does do, what he wants him to do. Whatever Jones's initial preferences and inclinations, then, Black will have his way. (Frankfurt 1969, 162)[3]

Suppose that Black wants Jones to rob a bank. Black installs a device in Jones such that, given a "triggering event" or "prior sign," the device activates, forcing him to rob the bank. Suppose also that Jones is morally responsible for robbing the bank since the action was up to him; the device in fact played no role. Yet given the device, Jones was unable to do otherwise. Thus, (3) is true and PAP is false. Or so the argument goes.

Frankfurt cases give rise to the "free will" crisis. We already had compelling reasons to accept (1) and (2) and Frankfurt cases offer a reason to accept (3). Note that the "free will" crisis is very different from the problem of free will. The "free will" crisis is a crisis about the meaning of "free will," not a crisis about the power of free will. The crisis is that, given Frankfurt cases, there is no general agreement about the meaning of "free will." As we have seen, some philosophers identify free will with sourcehood while others think that free will is the ability to do otherwise. Some think that free will is necessary for moral responsibility, others disagree. Some avoid the term "free will" altogether and focus on establishing freedom conditions for moral responsibility. Might there be a compromise among us? Something to satisfy the monist about free will as well as the pluralist about freedom? A core idea upon which both the fundamentalist and nonfundamentalist can agree? Our provisional view of free will is the compromise.

Free will is a power. There is some debate about whether it is a single, fundamental power or a collection of powers but there is universal agreement that it is a power associated with choice and action. All theorists should agree that an act is free if and only if it is or was up to the agent. This should offend neither the classical nor the source theorist. There is no denying that there is a debate about whether or not the ability to do otherwise is essential to moral responsibility. The debate comes down to a debate about the *classical thesis*: an act is up to an agent only if he is or was able to do otherwise (§ 1.2). Source theorists who reject the classical thesis, reject claim (2) of the "free will" crisis. Classical theorists who accept the classical thesis, reject claim (3) of the "free will" crisis. Neither should deny that free will is up-to-usness.

2.5   Moral Responsibility without Free Will

No matter how the fan of free will makes his case, someone is bound to object. Likely, we are always going to have free will skeptics, free will deniers. In the end this might not matter. If our interests in free will derive from our interests in moral responsibility, we might be able to do without free will. What is *necessary* in order for a person to be praiseworthy or blameworthy for an action? Suppose we left out the freedom condition. It would still be necessary that:

- The agent performs the act.
- The act is morally right or morally wrong.
- The agent is not ignorant about the particulars of the act.
- The agent has the relevant cognitive capacities and active powers.

The story of moral responsibility could be told without talking about free will at all.

On the other hand, we could think of free will just as the set of powers relevant to moral responsibility. Perhaps they are a collection of powers or perhaps they are the fundamental powers – such as the ability to do otherwise or the power to act – lurking behind the conditions noted above. Even Kane (1996; Fischer, Kane, Pereboom, and Vargas 2007) notes that the ability to do otherwise, in the form of a tracing principle, is necessary for ultimate sourcehood. Again, it is open to a classical theorist to accept that the ability to do otherwise is essential precisely because free will requires up-to-usness. For up-to-usness requires the ability to do otherwise, in turn.

Further Reading

Van Inwagen (1983) is a classical incompatibilist. For compelling versions of classical compatibilism, see Lehrer (1990) and Vihvelin (2004); for interesting versions of source compatibilism, see Frankfurt (1988), Fischer (1994) and Fischer and Ravizza (1998). Pereboom (2001) is a source incompatibilist worth looking at.

Many of the essays discussed in this chapter are contained in Fischer (1986a) and Fischer and Ravizza (1993a). The introductions to these anthologies – Fischer (1986b) and Fischer and Ravizza (1993b), respectively – are worth exploring, as well. The literature on Frankfurt (1969) cases is enormous but Fischer (1999) and Pereboom (2000), both reprinted in part in Kane (2002a), provide excellent summaries of the contemporary debate. For a pluralist take on the "free will" crisis, see Balaguer (2010).

Films about Moral Responsibility

- *"M"* (Fritz Lang, 1931)
- *North by Northwest* (Alfred Hitchcock, 1959)
- *Memento* (Christopher Nolan, 2000)
- *Minority Report* (Steven Spielberg, 2002)
- *A Clockwork Orange* (Stanley Kubrick, 1971)
- *Crimes and Misdemeanors* (Woody Allen, 1989)
- *Mother Night* (Keith Gordon, 1996)
- *Breathless* (Jean-Luc Godard, 1960)
- *Vertigo* (Alfred Hitchcock, 1958)
- *Lost Highway* (David Lynch, 1997)

3
The Problem of Free Will

In the previous chapter we considered several necessary conditions for moral responsibility and concluded that, given our provisional understanding, free will is necessary for moral responsibility as well. Here we consider arguments for free will skepticism and related theses. In the next chapter (Ch. 4) we consider similar arguments about moral responsibility.

The free will dilemma is best understood as an argument for free will skepticism. Here is the **free will dilemma** noted earlier (§ 1.5).

1. If determinism is true, then no one has free will.
2. If indeterminism is true, then no one has free will.
3. Therefore, no one has free will.

First, we explore arguments for premise (1), the first horn of the free will dilemma (§ 3.1–2). In particular, we investigate two formal versions of the consequence argument. Next, we explore arguments for the second horn of the dilemma, premise (2), stemming from the problem of luck (§ 3.3). Finally, we consider the best contemporary version of the free will dilemma (§ 3.4).

3.1 The First Argument

The **consequence argument** is an argument for *incompatibilism*, the claim that the free will thesis is inconsistent with the thesis of determinism.

> If determinism is true, then our acts are the consequences of the laws of nature and events in the remote past. But it is not up to us what went on before we were born, and neither is it up to us what the laws of nature are. Therefore, the consequences of these things (including our present acts) are not up to us. (van Inwagen 1983, 16)

Note that the argument is characterized in terms up-to-usness. Nonetheless, versions of the argument usually presuppose the classical view of free will, and that is the interpretation that we adopt.

Van Inwagen provides three formal versions of the consequence argument (1983, Ch. III). He notes that "the principle of individuation of arguments is far from clear" (56) and that "if there were some fundamental mistake *common* to all three arguments, it would be at least *likely* to reveal itself in one of them, however well hidden it was in the others" (57). We consider these to be three formal versions of the same argument – the consequence argument – informally expressed above.

In the next two sections of this chapter, we explore two formal versions of the consequence argument: the *first* (or *main*) *argument* (1975; 1983, 68–78)[1] and the *third argument* (1983, 93–104; 1989, 404–405; 2000). For the first argument, consider this example from van Inwagen:

> Let us suppose there was once a judge who had only to raise his right hand at a certain time, T, to prevent the execution of a sentence of death upon a certain criminal, such a hand-raising being the sign, according to the conventions of the judge's country, of a granting of special clemency. Let us further suppose that the judge – call him 'J' – refrained from raising his hand at that time, and that this inaction resulted in the criminal's being put to death. We may also suppose that the judge was unbound, uninjured, and free from

paralysis; that he decided not to raise his hand at T
a period of calm, rational, and relevant deliberatic
had not been subjected to any 'pressure' to decide
or the other about the criminal's death; that he was i
the influence of drugs, hypnosis, or anything of t
and finally, that there was no element in his deliberations
that would have been of any special interest to a student of
abnormal psychology. (van Inwagen 1975, 190–191)

Given the above together with determinism, van Inwagen
attempts to show that the judge was unable to raise his hand
at T; he could not have done otherwise.

Let "J" denote the judge, "T" denote the time that he
should have raised his hand, "T_0" denote an instant prior to
J's birth, "P_0" denote the proposition that expresses the state
of the world at T_0, "P" denote the proposition that expresses
the state of the world at T, and "L" denote the conjunction
of laws of nature. Here is the first argument:

1. If determinism is true, then the conjunction of P_0 and L
   entails P.
2. If J had raised his hand at T, then P would be false.
3. If 2 is ture, then if J could have raised his hand at T, J
   could have rendered P false.
4. If J could have rendered P false, and if the conjunction
   of P_0 and L entails P, then J could have rendered the
   conjunction of P_0 and L false.
5. If J could have rendered the conjunction of P_0 and L false,
   then J could have rendered L false.
6. J could not have rendered L false.
7. If determinism is true, J could not have raised his hand
   at T. (1975, 191)

There are several interesting replies to this argument.

One approach is to adopt a **weak view of laws** of nature,
aka *Humeanism* about laws of nature (Beebee and Mele
2002; Perry 2004). According to the weak view of laws, laws
are true *because* of the events that occur. If things had gone
a little differently, then the laws would have been different.
This is contrasted with a **strong view of laws**, where "the
truth of laws [is] established by something else, so that events

conform to them because they are laws" and not vice versa (Perry 2004, 237). Proponents of the weak view reject premise (6) of the first argument. The laws are what they are in part *because* we do what we do. If I had done otherwise, the laws would have been different (cf. Westphal 2003). Given this weak view of laws, I could have altered the laws merely by doing something else. Hence, the laws are no imposition on my ability to do otherwise.

Both David Hume (1975) and David Lewis (1986, ix) adopt the weak view of laws but these philosophers offer more compelling reasons for rejecting the consequence argument and defending compatibilism than a weak theory of laws. Hume's views are not discussed in this book, though P. F. Strawson's view is similar (§ 5.4). Lewis notes that the term "render" is ambiguous. Recall our previous examples of *rendering*: I am able to raise my hand, thereby rendering it true that my hand is raised; or I can leave my hand by my side, thereby rendering it false that my hand is raised. According to Lewis, I was able to **render a proposition false in the strong sense** if I was able to do something such that the proposition would have been falsified by my action or a consequence of my action. Whereas, I was able to **render a proposition false in the weak sense** if "I was able to do something such that, if I did it, the proposition would have been falsified (though not necessarily either by my act, or by any event caused by my act)" (120). Given the weak sense of "render," which Lewis favors, one should deny premise (6) but given the strong sense of "render" one should deny premise (5) (120). Either way, the first argument is unsound. What's nice about this response is that one can deny premise (6) without adopting Humeanism about laws of nature.

Keith Lehrer (1980) provides a related response to the first argument. He writes: "If S had done A at t [where S is a person, A is an action, and t is a time], then, of course, either the laws of nature would have been different or the state of the universe would have been different. But that is not to say that the person could have brought about these conditions." The Lehrer/Lewis response recognizes that, given determinism, my actions are the consequence of the laws and past events. Nonetheless, my ability to do otherwise does not require a subsequent ability to render the laws or the past false in the strong sense. It only requires an ability to render them false in the weak sense.

John Perry (2004) takes a different approach. Perry contrasts two different theories of *ability*. Consider first the **incompatibilist view of ability**, which is spelled out nicely in these quotes:

- . . . *freedom is freedom to add to the given past* (Ginet 1990, 102–103).
- . . . an agent can do X only if his doing X can be an extension of the actual past, holding the laws fixed (Fischer 1994, 88).
- . . . it *seems* that our freedom can only be the freedom to add to the actual past; . . . to act in accordance with the laws of nature (van Inwagen 2000, 167).

If determinism is true, then there can only be one "extension of the actual past, holding the laws fixed." Given the incompatibilist view of ability it is no wonder that determinism entails free will skepticism.

Perry distinguishes between strong and weak theories of ability. The **strong theory of ability** endorses the following principle:

- If x can perform A at t, then at no time earlier than t is it settled whether x performs A at t (Perry 2004, 241).

The **weak theory of ability** rejects the above principle. A proposition is **settled** if and only if it is entailed by some set of propositions about the past together with the laws of nature. Given determinism, all propositions about the future have been settled. The incompatibilist view of ability is a strong theory of ability. Perry adopts a weak view of ability and denies premise (4) of the first argument (241ff.).

According to van Inwagen, premise (4) – If J could have rendered P false, and if the conjunction of P_0 and L entails P, then J could have rendered the conjunction of P_0 and L false – is supported by a more general principle:

(S) If S can render R false, and if Q entails R, then S can render Q false (1975, 192).

Principle (S) has some intuitive appeal but Perry (2004, 247) shows that it is invalid, for it is subject to a counterexample. Here is a slightly amended version of Perry's counterexample. Let R be the proposition *that Joe raises his hand at* t, where *t* is some future time. Let Q be a conjunction: *that Joe raises his hand at* t & *that Joe's mother ate a cookie in 1950*. Note that Q includes R as one of its conjuncts. Thus, Q entails R. Suppose also that Joe's mother did *not* eat a cookie in 1950. Presumably, Joe can render R false by not raising his hand at *t*. Q entails R but Joe cannot render Q false since Q was rendered false by his mother in 1950.

The first argument utilizes the invalid inference rule (S), so the argument is not sound. The argument might be repaired with a new and better inference rule. And this would be worth discussing were it not for the fact that there is a better version of the consequence argument available, the third argument (1983, 93–104, 1989 and 2000).

3.2 The Third Argument

In the third argument, van Inwagen employs the **N-operator**, where "Np" stands for "p and no one has, or ever had, any choice about whether p" (1989, 404). For our purposes, one has a choice about whether p iff one is able to render p false provided that it is ture (1983, 66–7). Van Inwagen then claims that according to the logic of the N-operator the following two inference rules are valid:

(α)   From $\Box(p)$ deduce N(p);

(β)   From N(p) and N($p \rightarrow q$) deduce N(q),

where "$\Box(p)$" stands for "p is broadly logically necessary" and "$p \rightarrow q$" stands for "if p, then q" (1989, 227; 1983, 94). Roughly, a proposition is **broadly logically necessary** if and only if it is true in all (metaphysically) possible worlds. According to principle (α), given that something is broadly logically necessary it follows that it is true and no one has or ever had a choice about whether it is true. Thus, given that it is broadly logically necessary that $1 + 1 = 2$ it follows that it is true and no one has or ever had a choice about whether $1 + 1 = 2$ is true. Principle (β) is more difficult to explain but essentially it transfers the inability to render a proposition false onto other propositions: if you have no choice whether a proposition is true (for instance, if it is true yet you are unable to render it false) and you have no choice whether the proposition is true only if some other proposition is true, then you have no choice whether the other proposition is true.

Given principles (α) and (β), together with reasonable assumptions about the past and the laws of nature, one can show that if determinism is true, then no is or ever was able to render any true proposition false. Let P_0 be any true proposition about the **remote past**, that is the time "before there were any human beings" (1989, 224; Finch and Warfield 1998). Let L and P be as above. Here is the third argument (1983, 93–104; 1989, 404–405; 2000).

(1)	$\Box((P_0 \,\&\, L) \to P)$	assumption of determinism
(2)	$\Box\,(P_0 \to (L \to P))$	from (1) by exportation
(3)	$N(P_0 \to (L \to P))$	from (2) by (α)
(4)	$N(P_0)$	assumption
(5)	$N(L \to P)$	from (3), (4) by (β)
(6)	$N(L)$	assumption
(7)	$N(P)$	from (5), (6) by (β)

One might wonder about principle (β) and, in fact, a decisive counterexample to (β) has been offered (McKay and Johnson 1996). However, this problem can be fixed in a variety of ways (van Inwagen 2000), for instance we could just replace (β) with the following:

(β') From $N(p)$ and (p entails q) deduce $N(q)$ (Widerker 1987; Finch and Warfield 1998; see also van Inwagen 2000).

According to principle (β'), the N-operator is *closed under entailment*. That is, if no one has a choice whether a proposition is true, and it entails another proposition, then no one has a choice whether the other is true either. There are no known counterexamples to principle (β'). Perry's counterexample to principle (S) rests on a false proposition: *that Joe's mother ate a cookie in 1950*. False propositions cannot be used to provide counterexamples to principles (β) or (β'), since $N(p)$ entails that p is true.

One might question premise (4) of the third argument, which claims that no one has or ever had a choice whether some proposition about the remote past – e.g. P_0 – is true (Campbell 2007). Two arguments may be given in support of premise (4).

(a) $N(P_0)$ because "no one can change the past" (1983, 92);

(b) $N(P_0)$ because P_0 is a true proposition about the remote past, a time "before there were any human beings" (1989, 224).

Argument (a) is unsound. Recall that "$N(p)$" stands for "p and no one has, or ever had, any choice about whether p." Let p be the proposition that Lillian did not eat a cookie in 1950. Perhaps it follows that Lillian *has* no choice about whether p – presumably there is nothing that she can do about it *now*. Yet it does not follow that Lillian never *had* a choice about whether p. Given that she was alive in 1950, there is no reason to think that she couldn't have eaten a cookie. Thus, the need for argument (b) (Campbell 2007).

The proponent of the third argument might argue that since P_0 describes the state of the world at a time prior to the existence of any human beings, no one has, or ever had, any choice about whether P_0. No one was around back then to have had such a choice. In argument (b), it is not the *pastness* of our past that gives it its necessity. Rather it is the *remoteness* of some of our past – the fact that our past continues back to a time prior to our existence. According to this argument, determinism is a threat to our free will only because there are true propositions about the remote past. It follows that the third argument cannot provide a general argument for incompatibilism. That there is a remote past is a *contingent* truth about the actual world, one that is not essential to the thesis of determinism. Similar comments apply to the first argument. In that argument there are no presuppositions about a remote past but there are assumptions about a **remote individual past**, for instance, a time prior to *J*'s existence (2007, 109).

There are two types of principles used in the third argument: **grounding principles**, which establish that there are true propositions about which no one has a choice (e.g. about the laws of nature or the past), and **transfer principles**, which transfer this lack of choice onto all true propositions. It is easy to derive the appropriate grounding principles given contingent features of the actual world, like the fact that there is a remote past. Yet that we have a remote past is not an essential feature of possible worlds in general. Nor is it an essential feature of deterministic worlds. Therefore, one popular line of reasoning in support of incompatibilism doesn't really prove incompatibilism. At most, it establishes a weaker thesis: Given determinism and *some contingent propositions about the world*, no one has free will (Campbell 2007, 2008b, and 2010).

Consider the example of *oscillating Adam*, who lives in a deterministic world, W*, where time is circular. There is no beginning or end to Adam's existence. He is in the grips of an everlasting, eternal recurrence. Adam spends his time growing "older" and getting "younger." He begins each cycle with powers comparable to the average 25-year-old and eventually develops powers comparable to the average 50-year-old. Then he slowly regresses back to the state at which he began, and the cycle starts all over again (cf. Campbell 2010).

There is no reason to think that oscillating Adam is impossible. But neither the first nor third argument can be used to show that Adam is unable to do otherwise in determined world W*, for W* has no remote past. In as much as versions of the consequence argument require a grounding principle about our lack of choice about propositions about the remote past, they cannot prove *incompatibilism*, the claim that the free will thesis is incompatible with determinism. This does not mean that these and other versions of the consequence argument are uninteresting or unimportant. But it does mean that the consequence argument fails as a proof of incompatibilism.

3.3 The *Mind* Argument

The consequence argument is an argument for the incompatibility between free will and determinism that is persuasive but not decisive. What about indeterminism? How realistic are the prospects for free will given indeterminism? This is the *problem of luck* and it leads us to the *Mind* argument. The *Mind* argument is so-named by van Inwagen (1983, 16) because influential versions of it were printed in the journal *Mind* (Hobart 1934, for instance). Van Inwagen is an incompatibilist but he considers three arguments for compatibilism (1983, Ch. IV), one of which is the *Mind* argument.

The *Mind* argument "occurs in three forms" or "three closely related strands" each of which has "a common beginning" (126). Van Inwagen adds that even though he is discussing arguments "for the compatibility of free will and determinism" the third strand of the *Mind* argument "is, strictly speaking, an argument for the *incompatibility* of free will and *indeterminism*" (148). He appeals to similar resources in an argument for **restrictivism**, the view that persons have "precious little free will" and "rarely, if ever, is anyone able to do otherwise than he in fact does" (1989, 405). The *Mind* argument is not a single argument with various formal versions, like the consequence argument. It is a collection of arguments centered on the problem of luck, and reasons for thinking that *in*determinism might harm or even destroy free will. Versions of the *Mind* argument offer a range of conclusions, from restrictivism to the incompatibility of free will and indeterminism. We are concerned only with those versions of the *Mind* argument that might lend support to premise (2) of the free will dilemma.

Van Inwagen offers an especially powerful version of the *Mind* argument. He also shows that the problem of free will remains no matter the underlying ontology. Some people think that free will requires **dualism**, the view that the mind, or soul, is a different kind of substance than the body and the rest of the material world. Consider, for instance, any arbitrary moment in a world of *immaterial angels*.

> ... either "the sheaf of possible futures" relative to each moment has only one member or it has more than one. If it has only one, the world of angels is deterministic. And then where is their free will? (Their freedom is the freedom to add to the actual past. And they can only add to the actual past

in accordance with the laws that govern the way angels change their properties and their relations to one another with time.) If it has more than one, then the fact that one possible future rather than another, equally possible, future becomes actual seems to be simply a matter of chance. And then where is their free will? (1998, 372)

The argument shows that the issue of the nature of substance isn't relevant. The problem of free will comes up even if we imagine a world full of immaterial angels. But does this argument lend support to premise (2) of the free will skepticism dilemma?

Van Inwagen claims that the *Mind* argument supports "the *incompatibility* of free will and *indeterminism*" (1983, 148). If indeterminism is true, it is "a matter of chance which becomes actual." Of course, van Inwagen is not really suggesting that the free will thesis is incompatible with the *denial* of determinism. He writes:

Incompatibilists maintain that free will requires indeterminism. But it should be clear even to them that not just any sort of indeterminism will do. Suppose, for example, that there is exactly one undetermined particle of matter somewhere in the universe, and that it is far from any rational agent, the rest of the universe being governed entirely by strict, deterministic laws. In that case, determinism is, strictly speaking, false. But, clearly, if determinism is incompatible with free will, so is the thesis that everything except one distant particle of matter is determined. (1983, 126)

Determinism entails that every act is determined by prior causes. Indeterminism does not entail anything about the causal structure of the world surrounding any particular human action. Thus, indeterminism cannot entail that every act is undetermined let alone that every act is a matter of luck. Ergo, the *Mind* argument does not support premise (2) of the free will dilemma (§ 1.5). Considerations of luck are relevant to free will skepticism but not for this reason. They are relevant because they lend support to the view that *indeterminism cannot help*. Free will is a mystery but "the requirement of indetermination will not suffice" to solve the mystery (Watson 1987a). The free will dilemma comes close but it is not a sound argument, for premise (2) is false. The free will dilemma loses on a technicality but a more powerful case for free will skepticism is offered in the next section.

3.4   Free Will Skepticism

A skeptic is someone who doubts what others believe to be true, but doubt comes in degrees. The agnostic and the atheist have their doubts about God's existence but the latter's doubts are more severe. The agnostic adopts *epistemological skepticism*. He holds that no one knows whether or not God exists. The agnostic might or might not be a believer but the atheist's doubt carries with it the explicit denial of God's existence. The atheist adopts *metaphysical skepticism*. The agnostic has doubts, to be sure, but they are mere doubts, not explicit denials.

Free will skepticism is a kind of metaphysical skepticism, for it is the claim that no one has free will. Free will skepticism is contrasted with two other theories: incompatibilism and impossibilism. The *incompatibilist* believes that the free will thesis is inconsistent with the thesis of determinism. According to the **impossibilist**, "it is *metaphysically impossible* for us to have free will, either because she thinks that our concept of free will is incoherent or because she thinks that free will is incompatible with some necessarily true proposition" (Vihvelin 2008; cf. G. Strawson 1986, 2002, 2004).

How are these three theses related: free will skepticism, incompatibilism, and impossibilism? Some connections are easy. For one thing, impossiblism entails both free will skepticism and incompatibilism. It entails free will skepticism yet not vice versa since the latter is merely a contingent thesis about the way the actual world happens to be whereas the former is a thesis about all (metaphysically) possible worlds. Furthermore, if free will is (metaphysically) impossible, it cannot co-exist with anything; ipso facto, it cannot co-exist with determinism and incompatibilism is true.

The thesis of free will skepticism is independent of determinism. Galen Strawson notes that free will skepticism "holds good whether determinism is true or false; the issue of determinism is irrelevant" (2002, 441). This means that there is a "determinism-independent argument" for free will skepticism (Strawson 1986, 84). We considered the free will dilemma but, technically, that argument was left wanting, for indeterminism is not *incompatible* with free will.

Strawson offers four versions of an "a priori" argument for free will skepticism called the "Basic Argument" (2002, 441–443; cf. 1986, 28–29; 2004). Here is Version 1:

1.1 When you act, you do what you do – in the situation in which you find yourself – because of the way you are.
1.2 If you do what you do because of the way you are, then in order to be URD for what you do you must be URD for the way you are.
1.3 You cannot be URD for the way you are.
1.4 Therefore, you cannot be URD for what you do (2002, 443).

"URD" is short for "ultimately responsible and deserving of praise or blame or punishment or reward" (cf. 442). Strawson's basic argument appears to be a *direct argument*, one that argues directly for incompatibilism about determinism and moral responsibility without presupposing anything about free will (§ 4.1).

According to Strawson, the basic argument "holds good whether determinism is true or false; the issue of determinism is irrelevant" (2002, 441). Version 1 is a "determinism-independent argument" for free will skepticism. After presenting Version 2, Strawson writes: "This argument goes through whether determinism is true or false, for we cannot be URD either way" (2002, 444).

Versions 3 and 4 (445–447 and 447–448, respectively) provide more detail. At the end of Version 4, Strawson writes:

Note that once again it makes no difference whether determinism is true or false. If determinism is false, it may be that some changes in the way one is are traceable to the influence of indeterministic or random factors. It is even possible that difficult decisions or efforts to change oneself may trigger indeterminsitic events in the brain. But indeterminsitic or random factors, for whose particular character one is *ex hypothesi* in no way responsible, cannot contribute in any way to one's being URD for the way one is. (2002, 448)

The argument is independent of determinism because even if determinism is false, it still seems that free will is threatened.

In the next chapter (§ 4.3), we consider Strawson's argument in another context, as an argument for skepticism about moral responsibility. But it is interesting to note that it may be taken as an argument for free will skepticism, as well. What is of particular interest is that, in contrast to the consequence argument, the focus here is on the source view of free will. Van Inwagen motivates a version of the problem of free will that might appeal to the classical theorist (§§ 3.1–3.3). But Strawson's argument takes source considerations into account.

We only note that the same kind of criticism given against the consequence argument (§§ 3.1–3.2) applies to this argument, as well. Add the possibility of eternal existence and you can't show that creatures lack free will, even if having free will requires their being *causa sui*. The argument hinges on the fact that there is a time at which we were not free and then uses a kind of transfer principle to argue that there is no point of time at which we can become free. But if you extend the individual's life into the eternal past and deny a first moment of existence, Strawson's skeptical conclusion cannot be reached. That tells us that there is something wrong with the argument since the length of our past should not matter to the issue one bit. If the past is over and done how could the length of my past matter to the issue of my current freedom? Yet why can't Strawson use these resources to prove that no one has free will even if we are eternal beings? After all, the concept of *causa sui* is supposed to be incoherent.

To be honest, my views about Strawson's argument are divided between thinking there is a clean criticism, like the one above, and thinking that the argument is sound. Perhaps the argument shows that free will as ultimate sourcehood is impossible. If that is the case, who cares? One might define "knowledge" as absolute infallible certainty. Given this definition, it is pretty easy to show that no one knows anything. But no one cares about that because we all accept that knowledge is fallible, that even the most certain of evidence does not guarantee truth. All this shows is that we don't have infallible knowledge but it doesn't follow from this that we don't know anything. Epistemologists have grown out of their infatuation with infallibility and learned to accept a concept of knowledge that is more fitting to actual human capacities. Part of me thinks that there is a solution to Strawson's argument but part of me thinks there isn't and that it only shows that free will theorists need to grow up, too, and reject the requirement of ultimate sourcehood.

Further Reading

Formal versions of the consequence argument have been offered by Ginet (1966, 1990), van Inwagen (1975, 1983, 1989, 2000), and Fischer (1994), though Fischer calls his argument "the basic argument." Forceful criticisms are provided by Lewis (1981), McKay and Johnson (1996) and Perry (2004). The most compelling versions of the *Mind* argument are also from van Inwagen (1983, 1989, 1998, 2000, 2004). See also Finch and Warfield (1998) and Nelkin (2001) for worthwhile discussions of the *Mind* argument. Van Inwagen (1983, 2004, 2008) and Strawson (1986, 2002, 2004) provide the best versions of the problem of free will.

4
Moral Responsibility: Incompatibilism and Skepticism

In this chapter, we consider three arguments: the direct argument, the manipulation argument, and the ultimacy argument. The *direct argument* attempts to establish **incompatibilism about moral responsibility**: the incompatibility between the **moral responsibility thesis** – the claim that someone is or was morally responsible for something – and the thesis of determinism. The direct argument is of interest to free will scholars for several reasons. First, it is formally similar to the third argument. The only difference is that the third argument adopts a *no-choice operator* – the N-operator – and the direct argument adopts a *non-responsibility operator*.[1] Second, the direct argument claims to be an argument for incompatibilism about moral responsibility that does not make any presuppositions about free will. Whether this is even possible should be of concern to free will theorists. Third, the direct argument might be useful to *source incompatibilists*, that is, incompatibilists about moral responsibility who reject the classical view of free will. A classical incompatibilist can argue for incompatibilism about moral responsibility via PAP and the consequence argument (Widerker 2002, 316) but this option is not open to the source incompatibilist. Perhaps the source incompatibilist can use the direct argument to argue for incompatibilism about moral responsibility. Later in this chapter (§ 4.1) we show that this option is not available.

The manipulation argument (§ 4.2) is an argument for incompatibilism about moral responsibility but the ultimacy argument is an argument for *skepticism about moral responsibility*. Unlike the direct argument, it is questionable whether either of these latter arguments is independent of presuppositions about free will. If one defines "free will" as the most fundamental power needed for moral responsibility, then one can easily turn the arguments below into arguments for incompatibilism or free will skepticism. In fact, Strawson's argument for free will skepticism (§ 3.4) is adapted from his argument for skepticism about moral responsibility, considered below (§ 4.3).

4.1 The Direct Argument

In Chapter 3, we studied the consequence argument, which rested on the classical view of free will. The direct argument argues more directly for *incompatibilism about moral responsibility*, without making assumptions about free will or even the freedom condition for moral responsibility. Another distinctive feature of the direct argument is that it incorporates a *non-responsibility transfer principle* like (β).

We begin with van Inwagen's (1980, 1983) version of the **direct argument**, with slight modifications from David Widerker (2002). This version utilizes two formal principles:

(A) From $\Box(p)$ deduce $NR(p)$;

(B) From $NR(p)$ and $NR(p \rightarrow q)$ deduce $NR(q)$,

where "$\Box(p)$" means "p is broadly logically necessary" and "$NR(p)$" means "p and no one is (now), or ever has been, morally responsible for the fact that p" (Widerker 2002, 317; cf. van Inwagen 1983, 184). According to principle (A), no one is (now), or ever has been, morally responsible for any claim that is broadly logically necessary. For instance, you are not morally responsible for the fact that $1 + 1 = 2$. Principle (B) is a non-responsibility transfer principle.

For van Inwagen's version of the direct argument, let P_0 be a proposition about the state of the world at some time in the remote past – a time prior to the birth of any human beings – and let L be the conjunction of laws of nature. P is any true proposition.

(1)	$\Box((P_0 \ \& \ L) \rightarrow P)$	assumption of determinism
(2)	$\Box(P_0 \rightarrow (L \rightarrow P))$	from (1) by exportation
(3)	$NR(P_0 \rightarrow (L \rightarrow P))$	from (2) by (A)
(4)	$NR(P_0)$	assumption
(5)	$NR(L \rightarrow P)$	from (3), (4) by (B)
(6)	$NR(L)$	assumption
(7)	$NR(P)$	from (5), (6) by (B)

Most criticisms of the direct argument focus on the validity of principle (B). Widerker (2002), for instance, provides persuasive counterexamples to (B) and other non-responsibility transfer principles. These counterexamples are of two kinds. One set mimics Frankfurt cases except for an important difference. In Frankfurt's original example there are two agents: the *intervener*, Black, and the **crucial agent**, Jones, who is deemed morally responsible but unable to do otherwise. In Widerker's first set of counterexamples to principle (B), there is only one agent and a *natural process* takes the place of the intervener. These are **single-agent Frankfurt cases**.

For instance, here is *erosion* (Ravizza 1994), a counterexample to principle (B) discussed by Widerker (2002) and in even more detail by Fischer (2004):

> Imagine that Betty plants her explosives in the crevices of a glacier and detonates the charge at T_1, causing an avalanche that crushes the enemy fortress at T_3. Unbeknownst to Betty and her commanding officers, however, the glacier is gradually melting, shifting, and eroding. Had Betty not placed the dynamite in the crevices, some ice and rocks would have broken free at T_2, starting a natural avalanche that would have crushed the enemy camp at T_3. (Widerker 2002, 318; cf. Ravizza 1994, 72–73).

Intuitively, Betty is responsible for the fact that the enemy camp is crushed at T_3 but no one is (now), or ever has been, morally responsible for the fact that "the glacier is gradually melting, shifting, and eroding" and no one is (now), or ever has been, morally responsible for the fact that, given that the glacier is melting, the enemy camp is crushed at T_3. This is a counterexample to principle (B), for consider this argument:

- NR(the glacier is melting)
- NR(the glacier is melting $\rightarrow$ the enemy camp is crushed at T_3)
- $\therefore$ NR(the enemy camp is crushed at T_3)

The premises of this argument are true but the conclusion is false, so it is invalid. Thus, principle (B) is invalid.

As Widerker notes (2002, 319), the proponent of the direct argument may respond to the failure of single-agent Frankfurt cases by strengthening (B):

(B$_1$)   From NR(p) and (p entails q) deduce NR(q) (Warfield 1996).

(B$_1$) is immune to Widerker's single-agent Frankfurt cases, so he turns to another set of examples. What is distinctive about this second set is that in each example the event that makes p true occurs after the event that makes q true. Nonetheless, q is a necessary condition for p. This alters the standard order in cases of causal determination. These are **altered chronology cases**.

Consider **bolt**, an altered chronology case suggested by Hud Hudson in correspondence.

> One day Sparky is born to two loving parents. Many years later, a bolt of lightning strikes Sparky and he dies soon after.

Now consider the following argument.

- NR(a bolt of lightning strikes Sparky)
- That a bolt of lightning strikes Sparky entails that Sparky exists.
- $\therefore$ NR(Sparky exists)

Sparky's parents were responsible for the fact that he exists even though no one is responsible for the fact that he was struck by lightning and that fact entails that Sparky exists. The above argument has true premises and a false conclusion, so principle (B$_1$) is invalid. Similar comments apply to Widerker's example *fate* (2002, 319).

The proponent of the direct argument might construct yet another non-responsibility transfer principle:

(B$_2$) From NR(p) and NR($p \rightarrow q$) deduce NR(q), where q describes an event or state of affairs that occurs later than that described by p. (Ginet 2002; Widerker 2002, 322 fn. 14)

This principle seems question begging. Why specify that the chronology of events should follow the order of worldly events unless one already has suspicions about determinism? Isn't the direct argument supposed to *justify* our suspicions of determinism? If one is already convinced that determinism is a problem for moral responsibility, why suspect that he would be persuaded by any supposed counterexample to principle (B$_2$) (cf. Widerker 2002, 322–323)?

Fischer (2004) argues that the debate about the validity of non-responsibility transfer principles like (B) eventually leads to a dialectical stalemate. According to Michael McKenna, a **dialectical stalemate** "arises when opposing positions within a reasoned debate reach points at which each side's arguments remain reasonable, even compelling, but in which argument runs out; neither can rightly claim decisively to have unseated the legitimacy of the other side's point of view" (2005; see also Fischer 1994, Ch. 4). Once a dialectical stalemate has been reached, it is futile to proceed further with the counter-example approach. For it will not lead to a resolution.

Even if Fischer is correct that disagreements about the soundness of the direct argument lead to a dialectical stale-mate, we might still question whether the direct argument can achieve its intended purpose of providing an argument for incompatibilism about moral responsibility that makes no presuppositions about free will. We show that there is a con-flict between accepting that some Frankfurt cases are genuine counterexamples to PAP and endorsing the kind of non-responsibility transfer principle needed for a sound version of the direct argument.

Suppose, for instance, that non-responsibility transfer principles like (B), (B$_1$), and (B$_2$) are valid inference rules. We show that given the validity of these principles, crucial agents in Frankfurt cases are not morally responsible for their actions. It follows that source incompatibilists cannot rely on both the plausibility of Frankfurt cases *and* the validity of non-responsibility transfer principles. In other words, the direct argument is not available as an argument for incompatiblism about moral responsibility to those source incompatibilists who are motivated by Frankfurt cases (Campbell 2006).

In order to make this point clearer, consider **tax evasion,**[2] a Frankfurt case from Derk Pereboom.

> Joe is considering claiming a tax deduction for the registration fee that he paid when he bought a house. He knows that claiming this deduction is illegal, but that he probably won't be caught, and that if he were, he could convincingly plead ignorance. Suppose he has a strong but not always overriding desire to advance his self-interest regardless of its cost to others and even if it involves illegal activity. In addition, the only way that in this situation he could fail to choose to evade taxes is for moral reasons, of which he is aware. He could not, for example, choose to evade taxes for no reason or simply on a whim. Moreover, it is causally necessary for his failing to choose to evade taxes in this situation that he attain a certain level of attentiveness to moral reasons. Joe can secure this level of attentiveness voluntarily. However, his attaining this level of attentiveness is not causally sufficient for his failing to choose to evade taxes. If he were to attain this level of attentiveness, he could, exercising his libertarian free will, either choose to evade taxes or refrain from so choosing (without the intervener's device in place). However, to ensure that he will choose to evade taxes, a neuroscientist has, unbeknownst to Joe, implanted a device in his brain, which, were it to sense the requisite level of attentiveness, would electronically stimulate the right neural centers so as to inevitably result in his making this choice. As it happens, Joe does not attain this level of attentiveness to his moral reasons, and he chooses to evade taxes on his own, while the device remains idle. (Pereboom 2003)

Recent surveys (Fischer 1999; Pereboom 2000) suggest that **genuine Frankfurt cases** – those Frankfurt cases that provide genuine counterexamples to PAP – must satisfy three conditions. Suppose that S does a, where S is the crucial agent of a Frankfurt case, the one who is morally responsible but unable to do otherwise. In every genuine Frankfurt case, these conditions hold:

(1) a is the result of one of two possible causal chains: c_1 (the actual, indeterministic causal chain) or c_2 (the counterfactual causal chain),

(2) a is the actual result of c_1 and thus it is the actual result of processes that are ultimately indeterministic, and

(3) S is the source of a. (Campbell 2006)[3]

In tax evasion, S is Joe, a is Joe's act of tax evasion, c_1 is the actual causal chain leading to Joe's action, and c_2 is the counterfactual causal chain that would have resulted had the neuroscientist's device sensed a moral reason with the specified force. Proponents of Frankfurt cases like tax evasion hold that (1) ensures that S was unable to do otherwise, (2) ensures that a was not the result of deterministic processes, and (3) ensures that a satisfies the freedom condition for moral responsibility.

There is a conflict between accepting that some Frankfurt cases are counterexamples to PAP and endorsing the kind of non-responsibility transfer principle needed for a sound version of the direct argument. In order to make the point more clearly, consider an agent-relative version of transfer principle (B) (cf. Fischer 1994, 8):

(B*)   From $NR_S(p)$ and $NR_S(p \rightarrow q)$ deduce $NR_S(q)$,

where "$NR_S(p)$" means "p and S is not (now) and never was morally responsible for the fact that p." Assuming conditions (1)–(3), one may demonstrate that if principle (B*) is valid, then crucial agents in Frankfurt cases are not morally responsible for their actions. Given (1)–(3), the crucial agent S in a genuine Frankfurt case is morally responsible for a even though he could not have done otherwise. In such examples, a is the result of one of two possible causal chains: c_1 (the actual, indeterministic chain that has its source in S) or c_2 (the counterfactual chain). Let C_1 be the proposition that c_1 is causally efficacious and results in S doing a, let C_2 be the proposition that c_2 is causally efficacious and results in S doing a, and let A be the proposition that S does a. Lastly "$p \lor q$" means "p or q."

In any genuine Frankfurt case, either c_1 or c_2 is causally efficacious and results in S doing a. Thus, $(C_1 \lor C_2)$ entails A, for S's doing a is part of the content of both C_1 and C_2. Given principle (A), it follows that no one is (now), or ever has been, morally responsible for the fact that if $(C_1 \lor C_2)$, then A (that is, no one is responsible for the fact that either c_1 or c_2 is causally efficacious, and that if this is so, a occurs). In particular, S is not responsible and $\text{NR}_S((C_1 \lor C_2) \to A)$. But S is not (now) and never was morally responsible for the fact that $(C_1 \lor C_2)$, since it is the intervener who ensures that either c_1 or c_2 is causally efficacious and results in a. From (B*) it follows that S is not (now) and never was morally responsible for the fact that A. The argument is perfectly general, so we can conclude that if (B*) is valid, then crucial agents in Frankfurt cases are not morally responsible for their actions.

There is no substantive reason for accepting (B) and denying its agent-relative counterpart, (B*) (cf. van Inwagen 1989, 408–409). Thus, the above comments suggest that, given (B), crucial agents in Frankfurt cases are not morally responsible for their actions. Moreover, for any genuine Frankfurt case there is a single-agent counterpart. Consider **tax evasion***, a single-agent version of tax evasion.

> Joe is choosing whether or not to cheat on his taxes and his psychology is such that in order to fail to evade taxes he must attain a certain level of attentiveness to his moral reasons. Joe also has a brain disorder such that whenever he attains this level of attentiveness, his brain is electrically stimulated so that he develops an irresistible inclination to cheat. In actual fact, Joe does not attend to his moral reasons but he chooses to cheat on his taxes anyway.

Given tax evasion* we have the following argument.

- NR(Joe has a brain disorder)
- NR(Joe has a brain disorder → Joe cheats on his taxes)
- ∴ NR(Joe cheats on his taxes)

Again, the premises of this argument are true but the conclusion is false. Single-agent Frankfurt cases undermine at least some of the transfer principles that are essential to versions of the direct argument.

One might argue that Joe in tax evasion* is not morally responsible for cheating on his taxes. Above we suggested that tax evasion* is a counterexample to principle (B) and now I am claiming that given principle (B) one may show that Joe in tax evasion* is not morally responsible for his action. In all honesty, I find it difficult to decide which way to go here. Yet this is consistent with my claim that there is a tension between accepting that Frankfurt cases provide counterexamples to PAP and endorsing the kinds of non-responsibility transfer principles needed for a sound version of the direct argument.

Similar comments apply to (B_1) and (B_2), for the differences between (B), (B_1), and (B_2) are irrelevant. Either tax evasion* is a counterexample to (B_1) and (B_2) or those principles may be used to show that crucial agents in Frankfurt cases, like tax evasion, are not morally responsible for their actions. Either way, the source incompatibilist motivated by Frankfurt cases cannot look to the direct argument to support incompatibilism about moral responsibility.

What should we conclude from all this? First, the direct argument is inconclusive, for it cannot provide a non-question-begging argument for incompatibilism about moral responsibility (Fischer 2004). Second, some if not all of the motivation for the direct argument is undercut since it is unhelpful to the source incompatibilist motivated by Frankfurt cases. Either way, the incompatibilist about moral responsibility is better off with another argument.

4.2   The Manipulation Argument

One version of the manipulation argument is Mele's *zygote argument* (2008, 279; see also 2006, 188–195).

> Diana creates a zygote Z in Mary. She combines Z's atoms as she does because she wants a certain event E to occur thirty years later. From her knowledge of the state of the universe

just prior to her creating Z and the laws of nature of her deterministic universe, she deduces that a zygote with precisely Z's constitution located in Mary will develop into an ideally self-controlled agent who, in thirty years, will judge, on the basis of rational deliberation, that it is best to A and will A on the basis of that judgment, thereby bringing about E. If this agent, Ernie, has any unsheddable values at the time, they play no role in motivating his A-ing. Thirty years later, Ernie is a mentally healthy, ideally self-controlled person who regularly exercises his powers of self-control and has no relevant compelled or coercively produced attitudes. Furthermore, his beliefs are conducive to informed deliberation about all matters that concern him, and he is a reliable deliberator. So he satisfies a version of my proposed compatibilist sufficient conditions for having freely A-ed.

Mele continues.

> Compare Ernie with Bernie, who also satisfies my compatibilist sufficient conditions for free action. The zygote that developed into Bernie came to be in the normal way. A major challenge for any compatibilist who claims that Ernie A-s unfreely whereas Bernie A-s freely is to explain how the difference in the causes of the two zygotes has this consequence. Why should that historical difference matter, given the properties the two agents share?

This is an argument for incompatibilism about moral responsibility. We need to look at the structure more deeply.

The manipulation argument contrasts **manipulation cases** – where an agent like Ernie is manipulated and presumed not to be morally responsible for his actions – with **determinism cases** – where the actions of agents like Bernie satisfy compatibilist necessary conditions for moral responsibility and are embedded in a deterministic world. The **no-difference claim** states that there is no substantive difference between these two kinds of examples. Therefore, the lack of moral responsibility in manipulation cases extends to determinism cases, and incompatibilism is true (McKenna 2008).

Soft-line replies to the manipulation argument reject the no-difference claim and contend that manipulation cases are distinct from determinism cases. Fischer claims that morally responsible actions need the right *history*. According to

Fischer and Ravizza (1998), an agent has *guidance control* just in case his behavior (action, choice, omission, etc.) issues from a moderately reasons-responsive mechanism that is the agent's own. Since this account requires *mechanism ownership*, and since, on his view, mechanism ownership obtains in (some) determinism cases but not in manipulation cases, Fischer is a **soft compatibilist**: He believes that some kinds of manipulation undermine an agent's moral responsibility. Thus, the action's *history* is important (see also § 5.3).

Michael McKenna (2008) has persuasively argued that soft compatibilism is doomed to failure, since better manipulation cases – ones that appear to be indistinguishable from determinism cases – are always forthcoming. *Hard-line* replies bite the bullet and accept the no-difference claim. However, they deny that all manipulation cases result in actions for which the agent is not morally responsible. Compatibilists who adopt the hard-line reply to the manipulation argument endorse *hard compatibilism* (McKenna 2008; Russell 2010). It bears noting that in some manipulation cases, the cognitive capacities of the agent seem to be hampered. Thus, one need not always take a hard-line approach (Mele 2008; Sripada manuscript). McKenna's point is more that, eventually, the compatibilist will be led to the hard-line approach, since manipulation cases can always be improved.

Pereboom's (1994) *four-case argument* for incompatibilism is also a version of the manipulation argument. It does not utilize a non-responsibility transfer principle and is not a version of the direct argument. In this argument, Pereboom offers three cases where it seems that an agent is manipulated in such a way that he is not morally responsible for his action. He then constructs a fourth case where determinism is true and suggests that the agent is not morally responsible for his action here either. There is no principled way, according to Pereboom, to distinguish the four cases. Our intuitions are explicable only if something like the "fundamental incompatibilist principle" (FIP) is true:[4]

> . . . if one's action results from a deterministic causal process that traces back to factors beyond one's control, to factors that one could not have produced, altered or prevented, then one is not free in the sense required for moral responsibility. (Pereboom 1994, 249; see also 246 and 252)

In order to best characterize this principle, let "NR_S" be the agent-relative non-responsibility operator noted in § 4.1 and let "$NC_S(p)$" mean "p and S has no control over the fact that p," where the term "control" is intended to designate the kind of freedom necessary for moral responsibility.

When I say that S has *no control* over the fact that p, I mean that the fact that p is not produced by S, cannot be altered by S, and cannot be prevented by S (Pereboom 1994, 249). More specifically, the fact that p is not produced by S if and only if p is a true proposition and S is not the source of the fact that p, and the fact that p cannot be altered or prevented by S if and only if p is a true proposition and there is nothing that S can do or could have done to make it the case that ~p. Thus, (FIP) may be characterized as follows:

(FIP₁) From $NC_S(p)$ and (p entails q) deduce $NR_S(q)$.

Given this principle, one can show that crucial agents in Frankfurt cases are not morally responsible for their actions, in the same way as previously demonstrated with principle (B*) (§ 4.1) (Campbell 2006).

What should we conclude from this? Do manipulation arguments establish incompatibilism about moral responsibility? First, manipulation does not always compromise one's moral responsibility, one's praiseworthiness or blameworthiness. Suppose that some radical rightwing nuts found out that Bill Clinton had a fondness for girls from Texas with big hair. Given this, they decided to manipulate him into having an affair with Monica Lewinsky. That alone wouldn't show that Clinton's actions were unfree. Nor would it show that he was not blameworthy for his actions. Second, in cases where manipulation wrecks freedom and control, it usually does so by undermining one's cognitive capacities. Thus, some soft-line responses to the manipulation argument are available. And if none of them work, there is always the hard-line response.

4.3 The Ultimacy Argument

One final argument for skepticism about moral responsibility is worth noting: the **ultimacy argument** (Strawson 2004, § 5; cf. Widerker 2002, 321).

- If determinism is true, then no one is the ultimate source of one's acts.
- One is morally responsible for one's acts only if one is their ultimate source.
- Therefore, if determinism is true, no one is morally responsible for one's acts.

According to Widerker, the truth of the first premise depends on a non-ultimacy transfer principle.

(BU) From $NU(p)$ and $NU(p \rightarrow q)$ deduce $NU(q)$,

where "$NU(p)$" means "p and no one is, or ever has been the ultimate source of its being the case that p" (Widerker 2002, 322).

Is (BU) valid? Can it be used by the source incompatibilist? Or may it be used to show that crucial agents in Frankfurt cases are not morally responsible for their actions? Consider tax evasion* (§ 4.1) and the following argument:

- $NU(C_1 \vee C_2)$
- $NU((C_1 \vee C_2) \rightarrow A)$
- Thus, $NU(A)$

Given that $(C_1 \vee C_2)$ entails A, the second premise is beyond repute, unless one wants to suggest that someone is the ultimate source of its being the case that some broadly logically necessary proposition is true. It is plausible that Joe is the ultimate source of its being the case that C_1 but it is not plausible that Joe or anyone else is the ultimate source of its being the case that $(C_1 \vee C_2)$. To suggest otherwise is to suggest that Joe is the ultimate source of its being the case that $(C_1 \vee \sim C_1)$, contrary to the spirit of (A) (§ 4.1).

What should we say about the conclusion? On the one hand, (BU) and the ultimacy argument have a great deal of intuitive force. This suggests that Joe is not morally responsible for cheating on his taxes in either tax evasion or tax evasion*. On the other hand, if we accept that tax evasion is a genuine Frankfurt case, then tax evasion* seems to be a counterexample to principle (BU). Either way, it is yet another problematic route for the source incompatibilist.

Randolph Clarke (2005) offers additional criticisms of the ultimacy argument. Here is how Clarke characterizes the argument, quoting Strawson (2005, 14):

- Nothing can be *causa sui* – nothing can be the cause of itself.
- In order to be truly morally responsible for one's actions one would have to be *causa sui*, at least in certain crucial mental respects.
- Therefore, nothing can be truly morally responsible.

In support of the second premise, Strawson offers the following:

1. You do what you do, in any situation in which you find yourself, because of the way you are.

    So

2. To be truly morally responsible for what you do you must be truly responsible for the way you are – at least in certain crucial mental respects. (Strawson 2002, 443)

For Clarke, the inference from (1) to (2) requires the following rule:

(O) When you do what you do because of the way you are, to be truly morally responsible for what you do, either (a) you must be truly responsible for the way you are, at least in certain crucial mental respects, or (b) it must be up to you whether if you are that way, in certain crucial mental respects, then you perform that action;

and

(P) When you do what you do because of the way you are, it is not possible for it to be up to you whether if you are that way, in certain crucial mental respects, then you perform that action. (Clarke 2005, 18–19)

Semicompatibilists and some source incompatibilists will reject (O).

In many respects, the issue comes down to a debate about sourcehood. Does moral responsibility require that the agent be the ultimate source of his actions? Or is it enough that we are adequate sources? This is a difficult question. On the one hand, perhaps ultimate sourcehood is analogous to *Cartesian certainty* in epistemology. We used to think that knowledge was absolute certainty. Eventually it became clear that under this understanding of knowledge, skepticism about knowledge quickly followed. We eventually gave up this view of knowledge and replaced it with a view where knowledge is *fallible* and something short of absolute certainty.

Likewise, if it turns out that ultimate sourcehood is impossible for the reasons that Strawson suggests, we could just let it go and try to focus on adequate sourcehood instead. After all, if it turns out that we lack free will because we lack a kind of sourcehood that is *impossible*, something that no person – not even God – could possibly have, how could that be such a great loss? Furthermore, there seems to be an assumption that a compatibilist theory of ultimate sourcehood is impossible, but that is far from clear as we see in the next section (§ 5.1).

Further Reading

Fischer (1982, 1986b, 1994, 2004), van Inwagen (1983), and Widerker (2002) are essential sources for the arguments in this chapter. The two best examples of the manipulation argument are from Pereboom (1994, 2001) and Mele (2006). McKenna (2008) offers a helpful response. The Strawson (1986, 2002, 2004) version of the ultimacy argument is worth perusing, as well as Clarke's (2005) response. The discussions by Fischer, Kane, Pereboom, and Vargas (2007) on these issues are worth exploring, as well.

5
Free Will Theories

Free will theories can be divided into three main camps. **Libertarianism** is the conjunction of incompatibilism and the free will thesis, which entails the denial of determinism. **Free will skepticism** is the denial of the free will thesis. **Compatibilism** is the view that the free will thesis is compatible with determinism. Incompatibilism is the denial of compatibilism and includes both libertarianism and free will skepticism. These views are considered in the next three sections (§§ 5.1–3), respectively. Each of these views engages with the problem of free will and arguments for free will skepticism. One might try to respond to the skeptic in a more subtle way and some *alternative views* are explored, as well (§ 5.4). We close with some final thoughts about free will (§ 5.5).

5.1 Libertarianism

The main libertarian theories can be distinguished in terms of broader theories of action (Clarke 2003, 2008; Ginet 1997). *Theories of action* can be divided into three different groups, based on two different kinds of considerations (Mele 1997b; Clarke 2003, 2008; Wilson 2009). First, we distinguish between causal and noncausal theories of action. According to the **causal theory** of action, explanations of actions are *causal explanations* whereas the **noncausal theory** of action holds that explanations of actions are not causal explanations. The noncausal theory – also called the "reasons-based view" or "noncausalism" – holds that actions are explained in terms of psychological items like beliefs, desires, and intentions. Yet while reasons of this sort might *explain* a person's actions, reasons are not *causes* of actions.

Second, among causal theories we can distinguish between the event-causal theory and the agent-causal theory. **Event-causal theorists** agree with noncausalists that the explanations of actions are reasons-based but unlike noncausalists they also believe that reasons are causes. **Agent-causal theorists**, on the other hand, agree with event-causal theorists that explanations of actions are causal explanations. However, while most philosophers think of causation as a relation between events, agent-causal theorists believe that some events are caused by *agents*. Agents are individuals, not events, and agents are the irreducible causes of their actions. Hence, agent causation is not reducible to event causation. Agents can be causes of events – they can cause their own actions or be causes of the consequences of their actions – but an agent is never the effect of another event or set of events. Libertarian causal theories are discussed within the context of a more detailed examination of noncausalism.

Carl Ginet (1989, 1990, 1997, 2002) offers the most fully developed noncausal theory of action, at least the most fully developed noncausalism from an *incompatibilist* perspective. I'm cheating a bit in classifying Ginet as a libertarian. He is a committed incompatibilist but, given the problem of luck and other matters, he is *agnostic* about the free will thesis. According to Ginet, every action is or begins with a basic action, or simple mental act (1990, 11) – a decision or a choice – and intentions, beliefs, desires, and so on explain but do not cause basic actions. Basic acts have an "actish phenomenal quality" (1990, 13) – *as if* the agents produced them – and this might give the mistaken impression that agents are causes. For Ginet, the agent *performs* but does not *cause* his action (1997, 208).

An important concern for Ginet is the problem of luck, as it is conveyed in the *Mind* argument (Ginet 1990, Ch. 6). Indeed, this problem seems to plague all libertarian theories.

Here is a version that seems to apply to almost any indeterministic theory:

> If a simple mental action of mine is uncaused, if it is in no sense determined to occur by anything at all, then it is not determined to occur by *me* in particular. But if I do not determine its occurrence, then it is not under my control. (O'Connor 1996, 146)

Ginet has an answer to this problem. He writes: "For an agent to determine whether or not an event, *e*, occurs is for her to make it the case that *e* occurs by performing some suitable free action" (1997, 208). Thus, a libertarian account of agent determination is open to the noncausalist. "Given that the action is free, the agent determines it, one could say, simply by being its subject, the one whose action it is. That is to say, all free actions are *ipso facto* determined by their subjects" (1997, 208). According to Ginet (1997, 2002, 2008), the noncausalist response to the problem of luck is better than the one provided by either the event-causalist or the agent-causalist. If he is correct, that would be a major reason for choosing noncausalism over the other libertarian theories.

Ginet holds a classical view of free will: "an action is free if and only if up until the time of the action the agent had it open to her not to perform it; she could then have performed some other action instead or not acted at all" (1997, 207; cf. 1990, 124). He is also an incompatibilist: free will and free action are incompatible with determinism. In fact, Ginet offers the first formal version of the consequence argument (1966) and his most recent version (1990, Ch. 5) is intriguing though it hasn't received its deserved attention. Ginet also endorses something close to PAP: "an agent can be morally responsible for her action only if it is a free action" (1997, 207; see also 1996). Since Ginet accepts the classical thesis (1990, 90), PAP follows.

Noncausalism is not an essentially incompatibilist or libertarian theory. For instance, here is a neo-Kantian noncausalist compatibilist view.[1] Every action has both a **causal explanation,** in terms of past events and the laws of nature, as well as a **practical explanation,** in terms of the agent's beliefs and desires. Whether the action is *determined* is settled by the details of the causal explanation but whether the action is *free* is settled by the details of the practical explanation, which is a noncausal, reasons-based explanation (Wood 1984). Thus, the problem of free will and determinism is a kind of *category mistake*.

The success or failure of neo-Kantianism might depend on one's views about ultimate sourcehood. For instance, earlier we noted that we can distinguish between two kinds of ultimate sourcehood theorists (§ 1.1). Some ultimate sourcehood theorists believe that it is only necessary that persons are the ultimate sources of their actions. Others add that the actions cannot have any prior causes or influences outside of the agent. Of course, this last condition rules out compatibilist theories from the start, or at least all of the compatibilist theories we are considering. You would think that being an ultimate cause was enough. At least you would think so unless you thought that determinism ruled out genuine free will. But doesn't that just get us back to the consequence argument?

Whether or not one's theory of action is committed to incompatibilism is going to be settled by other factors, like the soundness of the consequence argument or the soundness of the manipulation argument or the plausibility of classical compatibilism. Ginet understands this as well as anyone. Similarly, in deciding between libertarian theories, one might ask how a particular theory stacks up against the problem of luck.

The *event-causal theory* – or "causal indeterminism" (Kane 2001, 239) or the "indeterministic causation view" (Ginet 1997, 208) or "event-causalism" – begins with Donald Davidson (1963), who was among the first contemporary philosophers to argue that reasons are causes. Davidson is a compatibilist but Robert Kane is an incompatibilist and a libertarian who adopts event-causalism. Kane's work is distinctive because it provides a libertarian theory that is rooted in a *naturalistic explanation* of the world, that is, one that does not appeal to any *supernatural* entities or powers. In other words, Kane provides a naturalist view of libertarian free will.

According to most contemporary philosophers and physicists, determinism is false. This is a complex and controversial issue. Several important surveys (Earman 2004; Hoefer 2010) note that there are consistent deterministic models of quantum mechanics. Nonetheless, most philosophers and physicists adopt an indeterministic interpretation of quantum mechanics. Indeterminism offers the libertarian the opportunity to ground free will in the natural world. Kane, perhaps more than any other philosopher, has taken advantage of this opportunity (1996, 2001, 2004; Fischer, Kane, Pereboom, and Vargas 2007).

Kane endorses *the condition of ultimate responsibility* (UR): "to be ultimately responsible for an action, an agent must be responsible for anything that is a sufficient reason (condition, cause or motive) for the action's occurring" (2001, 224; cf. 1996, 35).[2] This leads to Kane's definition of "free will": "the power to be the ultimate creator and sustainer of one's own ends or purposes" (2001, 223; cf. 1996, 4). One might expect that Kane adopts the source view but, like Ginet (1990), he adopts a classical view of free will. Kane (1996) accepts **the condition of alternative possibility** (AP), which requires that agents with free will can do otherwise. UR requires "that we could have done otherwise with respect to *some* acts in our past life histories by which we formed our present characters. I call these 'self-forming actions', or SFAs" (2001, 225; cf. 227–228). This leads to the adoption of a modified version of PAP: a person can have "ultimate moral responsibility" only if at least some of the actions in his "life history" could have been otherwise (1996, 42). Lastly, Kane thinks that moral responsibility, ultimate responsibility, and free will are all incompatible with determinism (1996, Ch. 4).

Central to Kane's theory is the concept of a *self-forming action*, or SFA. He writes: "SFAs occur at those difficult times of life when we are torn between competing visions of what we should do or become. . . . There is a tension and uncertainty in our minds about what to do at such times, I suggest, that is reflected in appropriate regions of our brains by movement away from thermodynamic equilibrium – in short, a kind of 'stirring up of chaos' in the brain that makes it sensitive to microindeterminacies at the neuronal level" (2001, 228). Thus, SFAs are indeterministic and this indeterminacy is tied to the physical world in a deep way. Though this explanation of human action appeals to the agent's reasons, intentions, beliefs, desires, it is both a *causal* and a *naturalistic* explanation, according to Kane.

To his credit, Kane considers several objections to libertarianism. To begin, there is the problem of luck, which Kane calls "the intelligibility question" (2001, 226). For instance, Timothy O'Connor asks: "how it can be up to *me* on a given occasion that certain of my reason states exert their indeterministic propensity to cause a decision to act, while others do not (though they might have done so)" (O'Connor 1996, 152)? He continues: "Doesn't it seem a matter of luck, the objection goes, that one of them overcame short-sighted temptation, while the other did not?" (1996, 155) Kane states the objection this way: "If the choice was undetermined, then exactly the same deliberation, the same thought processes, the same beliefs, desires, and other motives – not a sliver of difference – that led up to my favoring and choosing Hawaii over Colorado, might by chance have issued in my choosing Colorado instead" (2001, 226).

Kane has a response. Cases of practical deliberation are not paradigmatic of SFAs, in the way that moral or prudential choices are (1996, Ch. 9). In the former cases, indeterminism enters much earlier in the deliberation process. This is why it would be absurd for one to choose Colorado given that reason favors Hawaii.[3]

Mark Balaguer (2010) develops a libertarian theory modeled off of Kane's view. He makes it clear that he is just developing the theory and not necessarily endorsing it (69). It has two essential and interrelated parts. One is **TDW-indeterminism**, the thesis that "Some of our torn decisions are *wholly undetermined* at the moment of choice" (78). The other is the concept of a *torn decision*. Balaguer claims that "if our torn decisions are wholly undetermined in the manner of TDW-indeterminism," then they are L-free (or libertarian free) because "(a) they are sufficiently rational to count as L-free; (b) we author and control them; (c) the indeterminacy increases or procures the authorship and/or control; and (d) the indeterminacy-enhanced authorship and control that we get here is worth wanting" (119). Thus, L-freedom is a freedom worth wanting that is essentially indeterministic. Balaguer doesn't commit to the claim that

L-freedom is required for moral responsibility, but he says that if we have L-freedom, then we have the kind of freedom we need to be morally responsible for our actions. Whether we have L-freedom boils down to the empirical question of whether our torn decisions are undetermined in the right way.

Torn decisions have two main phenomenological components. First, the agent "has reasons for two or more options and feels torn as to which set of reasons is strongest, that is, has no conscious belief as to which option is best, given her reasons." In addition, the person "decides without resolving this conflict – that is, the person has the experience of 'just choosing'" (71). Torn decisions are opposed to *Buridan's-ass decisions*, where "the reasons for the various tied-for-best options are the *same* reasons" (72): equal desires for two piles of hay, for instance. In these cases "the agent doesn't feel torn as to which option is best" (73). Torn decisions are similar to Kane's SFAs but there are several differences worth noting (73ff.).

The key is that torn decisions are such that "If they are undetermined at the moment of choice . . . then they are L-free" (68). This is because if our torn decisions are undetermined in the right way, they are (a) "appropriately non-random" and (b) "the indeterminacy in question increases or procures the appropriate nonrandomness" (68). Balaguer claims that "if our torn decisions are undetermined at the moment of choice, then (a) and (b) *are* true" (69). It is for this reason that "the question of whether libertarianism is true just reduces to the question of whether some of our torn decisions are undetermined in the appropriate way" (69), an empirical question "about whether certain neural events are undetermined" (70).

Libertarian event-causal theories also suffer from *the problem of contrastive explanations* (cf. Ginet 1997, 214). A *contrastive explanation* is something of the form "c causes e rather than e^*" where c, e, and e^* are all events. Let e be the event of the judge raising his hand and let e^* be the event of the judge keeping his right hand near his side. Suppose that e is an SFA that is explained by c. In other words, that c caused e explains why e occurred. Since e is the act of the judge raising his hand (or some more basic act, such as the judge trying or intending to raise his hand), that *c* caused *e* explains why the judge raised his hand. Nonetheless, although *c* causes *e*, *c* does not causally determine *e*. Even if one accepts that *c* caused *e* explains why *e* occurred, there is absolutely no contrastive explanation for why the agent did *e* and not *e**. This gets us back to the problem of luck.

Lastly, we consider the **agent-causal view**, also called "agent-causalism" or the "agency theory" or even the "libertarian agency theory." This view of free will has been around at least since the eighteenth-century Scottish philosopher Thomas Reid (1983). In the twentieth century, C. A. Campbell (1951, 1957), Richard Taylor (1963), and Roderick Chisholm (1964) set forth a revitalization of the agent-causal view that is still going strong (O'Connor 2000, Clarke 2003). We begin with the *traditional libertarian agency theory*, which has five essential features (cf. Clarke 1996, 274–6).

1. Agent causation is a relation between a person (the *agent*) and an event (the *action*).
2. Agents are causes of their actions but this causal relation is not reducible to event causation; agents are not events or sets of events.
3. Agents are not caused to act by anything, for only events can be caused.
4. Actions that are agent-caused are not determined, that is, they are not the consequences of past events together with the laws of nature.
5. An action that is agent-caused has no event cause.

Consider the features of the traditional libertarian agency theory more closely.

According to feature (1), causes of actions can be *agents*, not just events. Usually, causation is understood as a relation between events, so the idea of something other than an event playing a causal role is odd to many philosophers. Nonetheless, according to feature (2), agent causation allows for a *primitive relation*, one that is not reducible to some set of event-causal relations. As feature (3) notes, agents can cause but cannot be caused, so their role in the *causal nexus* – that is, their role in the complete history of worldly events – is limited. Feature (4) is just the requirement of indeterminism, essential to any libertarian theory.

Randy Clarke parts ways with the traditional libertarian agency theory when it comes to feature (5). According to feature (5), agents are always the *complete cause* of their actions. Given feature (5), every free action is like an SFA. This is problematic not only because of the luck objection – for on this view it is unclear what "free" means other than "not determined" and thus "random" – but also because it fails to explain how worldly events influence what we do. Without telling the *whole story*, as in the case of determinism, feature (5) leaves the explanation of our actions isolated from the world and its influence. It suggests that free acts are either rare (Campbell 1951, 1957; cf. van Inwagen 1989) or mysterious and inexplicable (Chisholm 1964). Neither is a good result.

Clarke seeks to better integrate human actions within the causal nexus while maintaining the sovereignty of the agent. His compromise is to accept features (1)–(4) while rejecting feature (5). According to this **new libertarian agency theory**, agents cause their free actions but agents themselves are not effects. Actions are influenced by agents but are also the effects of other events. We cause our own actions but things that happen in the world around us also influence what we do. Of course, everyone accepts claims like these but Clarke's view accommodates them better than previous libertarian agency theories.

Unfortunately, agent causal theories are subject to the problem of contrastive explanations, too. As Ginet puts it: "the agent *per se* cannot *explain* why the event happened precisely when it did rather than at some slightly different time. . . . Nor . . . can the agent *per se* explain why that particular sort of event rather than some other sort happened just then" (Ginet 1997, 214). Ginet's first example contrasts the same type of event occurring at either of two different times, while the second example is closer to the example above. Even Clarke acknowledges the force of this objection: "Whether such an action is agent-caused or not, there will be no contrastive rational explanation for it, one that would answer the question, 'Why did you choose this apple rather than that one?'" (1993, 206)

Just as Clarke supposes that feature (5) is not relevant to the agent-causal theory, one might equally question the importance of feature (4). Ned Markosian (2002) puts forth a **compatibilist theory of agent causation**, which is like Clarke's new theory of agent causation but for its rejection of feature (4). This provides an interesting objection to libertarian theories. For all libertarian theories are susceptible to the problem of luck. That problem, though, is apparently solved by compatibilism, since the compatibilist can account for contrastive explanations. Some combination of Markosian's view and the neo-Kantian view noted above might be just what the compatibilist is looking for.

In closing, we put forth **neo-existentialism**. Suppose the world contains two fundamentally different *aspects* of reality: the for-itself and the in-itself (Sartre 1956; Levy 2002). The *for-itself* is based on our understanding of the world from the subjective perspective, as a world containing free agents. The *in-itself* is based on our understanding of the world from the objective perspective, as nothing but matter and the void. For each aspect, there is a unique way of explaining worldly events. **Event-based explanations** explain every event by reference to complete descriptions about the world together with laws of nature. **Agent-causal explanations** of all actions can be given from the aspect of the for-itself. Beliefs and desires *influence* our actions but explanations of action are not reducible to our *facticity*; they are not reducible to the set of facts about us. This includes our beliefs and desires as well as the particulars about our circumstances. Event-based explanations and agent-causal explanations are both *causal explanations* but they are different kinds of causal explanations, understood from different aspects. The one explanation is not reducible to the other.

Of course, there is nothing about this story that tells against libertarianism. At most one can give an *Ockham's razor* type of objection: any theory that requires incompatibilism is more complex than a theory that does not, for it requires one further necessary condition. Thus, all things being equal, one should adopt compatibilism over libertarianism. But this depends on the fact that all things are equal, that none of the arguments for incompatibilism and incompatibilism about moral responsibility are sound.

5.2 Free Will Skepticism

From the enlightenment until the twentieth century, most philosophers were determinists. Thus, the most popular form of free will skepticism was *hard determinism*: determinism is true yet determinism is incompatible with free will, so no one has free will. One of the earliest proponents of this view was the seventeenth-century philosopher Baruch Spinoza. Spinoza was a *monist* in two different respects. First, he was a monist as opposed to a dualist. Spinoza thought that there was only one *kind* of substance, contrary to *dualism*, which asserts that there are two kinds of substances: souls and bodies. Second, Spinoza was a monist as opposed to a *pluralist*, for he thought that there was only one particular substance and not *many*, as the pluralist believes. The one substance can be understood through either of two attributes. Understood through the attribute of *thought*, we call that substance "God" but understood through the attribute of *extension* – the property of *being extended in space* – it is perhaps better called "Nature." In addition to being a free will skeptic, Spinoza was a pantheist, that is, he literally believed that God was everything and everything that was not God was a modification of God's *attributes*, or essential properties (1677, a1).

Spinoza adopted determinism as well as **necessitarianism**, the view that every true proposition is necessarily true (Bennett 1984; Garrett 1991). Spinoza's argument for incompatibilism is short and sweet:

- "That thing is called free which exists from the necessity of its nature alone, and is determined to act by itself alone" (Spinoza 1676, I.d7)
- "God alone is a free cause" (p. 17)
- Therefore, nothing else can "be called a free cause but only a necessary one" (p. 32).

Every event that happens and every true proposition necessarily follows given the nature of God, who necessarily exists (p. 11) and whose attributes are equally necessary (d4). Here is Spinoza's most famous quote about free will:

> ... men think themselves free, because they are conscious of
> their volitions and their appetite, and do not think, even in
> their dreams, of the causes by which they are disposed to
> wanting and willing, because they are ignorant of [those
> causes]. (I.Appendix)

Though human beings lack free will – which requires *ultimate sourcehood*, according to Spinoza – human beings can still obtain *blessedness*, which is a kind of freedom. When the cause of an action lies within the agent and his own knowledge, he is the *adequate cause* of his actions; otherwise he is merely a *partial cause* (Nadler 2009). **Blessedness** is the state at which one becomes the adequate cause of all of his actions.

Since the advent of quantum mechanics, few contemporary philosophers adopt determinism let alone necessitarianism. Nonetheless, Ted Honderich endorses determinism and rejects the free will thesis because of determinism (1988, 2002, 2004). In "After Compatibilism and Incompatibilism" (2002), Honderich argues strongly for the startling thesis that both compatibilism and incompatibilism are wrong![4] Each claims that we have one settled conception of free will, or one important conception of the kind of freedom needed for moral responsibility, and this, he argues, is demonstrably false. Like Richard Double (1996), Honderich suggests that the concept of free will is incoherent, for some of the reflections on our past lives convey a confidence in determinism but some give rise to views about moral responsibility that seem to depend on indeterminism.

We should take care in distinguishing between two closely related views. On the one hand, there is *free will skepticism*, which holds that no one has free will and the free will thesis is false. On the other hand, there is *impossibilism*, which claims that the free will thesis is *impossible*, not simply false (Vihvelin 2008). Similarly, a skeptic about moral responsibility believes that no one is morally responsible for anything but **impossibilism about moral responsibility** goes further in claiming that it is not possible for anyone to be morally responsible for anything.

Contrast, for instance, the views of Pereboom and Strawson. Pereboom is a **hard incompatibilist**, who holds that both determinism and the type of indeterminism that is most likely to be true are incompatible with the strongest freedom condition for moral responsibility (1994, 2001). Pereboom believes that libertarian agent causation is essential to moral responsibility and that nothing we definitively know rules it out. Yet, given the sort of indeterminism that is most likely to be true, there is no libertarian agent causation (2001, Chs 2 and 3). Since libertarian agent causation is possible (2006), Pereboom is a free will skeptic but not an impossibilist about free will and moral responsibility. Strawson, however, thinks that free will requires ultimate sourcehood but that ultimate sourcehood is incoherent. Thus, impossibilism.

Saul Smilansky is a free will skeptic but he differs from most free will skeptics in his endorsement of two "radical proposals" (2000). First, Smilansky is a partial compatibilist and endorses a "fundamental dualism" that attempts to combine the true but partial insights both of compatibilism and of hard determinism. Second, it is in general better to live under the *illusion* of free will than to embrace free will skepticism, for the consequences of free will skepticism (e.g. we cannot have true justice or deep moral worth) are too difficult to accept. This is **illusionism**.[5]

Unfortunately, the bad news about free will is not just that we don't have it. Smilansky argues that many contemporary philosophers have simply ignored the fundamental problem about our lack of ultimate control over our actions. The only way out is illusion. Van Inwagen (1998), following Chomsky and McGinn, has claimed that we might lack the cognitive skills needed to solve the free will problem, which would explain its persistence. Smilansky goes further in noting that our difficulty is in living with the problem, for the truth is too terrible to accept.

What are the consequences of free will skepticism? For some, they are not so dire as one might expect. Pereboom (2001) claims that, though nothing is *praiseworthy* or *blameworthy*, some things might be permissible or obligatory. Pereboom (2008) also thinks that deliberation is compatible with *belief* in determinism. Strawson believes that the acceptance of free will skepticism "is in no way incompatible with compassion" (1986, 120). Tamler Sommers (2007) believes that free will skepticism allows for love. Ben Vilhauer (2009) argues that free will skepticism does not undermine the basis for desert claims – judgments that someone is deserving of praise or blame. Perhaps the implications of free will skepticism are not as drastic as we first thought. On the other hand, such views might fail to accept fully the implications of a world without free will.

5.3 Compatibilism

Compatibilism is the view that the free will thesis is consistent with the thesis of determinism. This section discusses compatibilism in an even broader context. **Compatibilism about moral responsibility** is the view that determinism is consistent with the claim that someone is or was morally responsible for something (Ch. 4). Since there is debate over the meaning of "free will," not all compatibilists about moral responsibility are compatibilists. Recall (§ 2.2) that *semicompatibilism* holds that some freedoms – e.g. the ability to do otherwise – are incompatible with determinism but that moral responsibility is compatible with determinism. In this section we consider compatibilism as well as compatibilism about moral responsibility.

In the beginning the distinction between compatibilism and compatibilism about moral responsibility was irrelevant. Classical compatibilism was the dominant view among compatibilists until Frankfurt (1969). One influential proponent of classical compatibilism was G. E. Moore (1912). According to Moore, the argument for incompatibilism suffers from the *fallacy of equivocation*. Consider, this *short version* of the consequence argument (cf. 89).

1. If anyone has free will, then someone is able to do otherwise.
2. If determinism is true, then no one is able to do otherwise.
3. Thus, if determinism is true, then no one has free will.

Moore claims that the term "able" is ambiguous between the *categorical* and *hypothetical ability to do otherwise* (cf. 90–91).[6]

William James provides a wonderful illust[ ]
categorical ability to do otherwise. What does [ ]
that James – or anyone else – has a *genuine cho[ ]*
which way to walk home after one of James's lectures?

> It means that both Divinity Avenue and Oxford Street are
> called; but only one, and that one *either* one, shall be chosen.
> Now I ask you to seriously suppose that this ambiguity of my
> choice is real; and then to make the impossible hypothesis that
> the choice is made twice over, and each time falls on a differ-
> ent street. In other words, imagine that I first walk through
> Divinity Avenue, and then imagine that the powers that be
> annihilate ten minutes of time with all that it contained, and
> set me back at the door of this hall just as I was before the
> choice was made. Imagine then that, everything else being the
> same, I now make a different choice and traverse Oxford
> Street. (James 1956, 44)

The categorical ability to do otherwise is best understood in
terms of the relevant facts account (Campbell 2005). According to the *relevant facts account*, S is able to do otherwise
only if S's doing otherwise is compossible with the relevant
facts (cf. Lewis 1976 and 1979). The **broad past** is "the past
together with the laws of nature" (Finch and Warfield, 1998,
523). On one reading of this passage, James suggests that
having a choice entails having the ability to do otherwise
given the broad past. Let t be some time before S's choice –
for instance, some moment prior to the annihilation of time
noted above – and let Ψ_t be the set of propositions about the
broad past relative to t. If S has the categorical ability to do
otherwise, then that S does otherwise is consistent with Ψ_t.
This is **the incompatibilist criterion.**

The incompatibilist criterion is not an *analysis*, for it only
specifies a necessary condition for the ability to do otherwise.
Nonetheless, it identifies a central feature of the libertarian
or incompatibilist view of ability, e.g. Perry's *strong theory
of ability* (§ 3.1). G. E. Moore acknowledges that the **categorical ability** required by the incompatibilist criterion is
impossible given determinism. But he claims that this is not
the relevant kind of ability. In opposition, Moore contends
that "able" has two meanings and the consequence argument
is guilty of the fallacy of equivocation. Though Moore's

analysis is much more complex,[7] history has come to understand it in terms of the **hypothetical analysis:** "S was able to do otherwise" means "if S had willed (or chosen, or wanted, etc.) to do otherwise, then S would have done otherwise." **Hypothetical ability** is consistent with determinism, for it is only committed to the claim that, had things been different, different actions would have resulted.

Unfortunately, the hypothetical analysis is prone to clear and decisive counterexamples. Here is a famous counterexample from Keith Lehrer:

> It is logically possible that as a result of my not willing, not choosing, or not undertaking some action, I might lose any of my powers . . . Suppose that I am offered a bowl of candy and in the bowl are small round red sugar balls. I do not choose to take one of the red sugar balls because I have a pathological aversion to such candy. (Perhaps they remind me of drops of blood . . .) It is logically consistent to suppose that if I had chosen to take the red sugar ball, I would have taken one, but, not so choosing, I am utterly unable to touch one. I can take a red candy ball only if I so choose, but my pathological aversion being what it is, I could not possibly bring myself so to choose. I could do it only if I chose to, and I do not. (1968, 31–32)

It is true that if the individual in the above example had chosen to take a red candy, he would have taken one. Yet given that he was unable to make that choice, it seems to follow that he was unable to take a red candy. This is contrary to the hypothetical analysis, which suggests that the ability sentence is true whenever the corresponding conditional sentence is true.

Two results – the failure of the hypothetical analysis of "able" as well as the success of Frankfurt cases (§§ 2.2–2.4) – have led some compatibilists to abandon the classical view of free will and adopt *source compatibilism* instead. Two strands of source compatibilism, arguably the most influential strands, are worth discussing in detail. One understands the relevant kind of freedom as *reasons-responsiveness*. The other tries to spell out freedom in terms of *identification*.[8] Both strands of source compatibilism are developed by Fischer, so let's begin by discussing his views in more detail.

Fischer is a semicompatibilist and defends a version of the consequence argument (1994, Ch. 5). He also denies PAP and is in many ways aligned with the classical incompatibilist, for he agrees that the ability to do otherwise is incompatible with determinism. Since PAP is false, the ability to do otherwise is not necessary for moral responsibility. Fischer concedes that there is a kind of freedom or control that is incompatible with determinism, **regulative control**. Regulative control requires the ability to do otherwise. But regulative control is not necessary for moral responsibility. Fischer believes that the kind of freedom or control that is required for moral responsibility is *guidance control*, that guidance control is compatible with determinism, and that guidance control does not require the ability to do otherwise. Fischer is also a provocative critic of the direct argument (2004), discussed above (§ 4.1).

An agent has **guidance control** just in case his behavior issues from a moderately reasons-responsive mechanism that is the agent's own. Morally responsible action requires having the right history; it requires *mechanism ownership* (§ 4.2). Fischer is a *soft compatibilist*. The most salient freedom-relevant power necessary for moral responsibility, according to Fischer, is moderate reasons-responsiveness. **Moderate reasons-responsiveness** is a kind of guidance control that requires that "an agent act on a mechanism that is regularly receptive to reasons, some of which are moral reasons, and at least weakly reactive to reason" (Fischer and Ravizza 1998, 82). Moderate reasons-responsiveness seems to secure the appropriate connection between the agent and his action, that is, that the action is based on the agent's reasons. One benefit over classical theories, according to some, is that the link between agent and action is maintained without a commitment to the ability to do otherwise. We return to this issue shortly.

Several philosophers have focused on *identification*. For instance, there is the concept of *taking responsibility*. Frankfurt writes: "The question of whether the person is responsible for his own *character* has to do with whether he has *taken responsibility for* his characteristics. It concerns whether the dispositions at issue, regardless of whether their *existence* is due to the person's own initiative and causal agency, are characteristics with which he identifies and which he thus by his own will incorporates into himself as constitutive of what he is" (1987, 171–2). Similarly, Sartre (1956) talks about being responsible for your sexuality – whether you are gay or straight – in the sense that you can take responsibility for being one or the other, you can accept one of them as your own and not something that was merely given to you. This plays an important role in Fischer's view as well as well as Frankfurt's (1987).

Frankfurt (1969, 1971) is a main proponent of Susan Wolf's (1990) *deep self view*. Frankfurt distinguishes between first-order desires and second-order desires, which are desires about the kinds of first-order desires one wishes to have. For instance, I might have the first-order desire to have a hamburger. Perhaps my wife is a vegetarian and it disturbs her whenever I eat meat. In that case, I might also have a second-order desire not to have that desire. I might even attempt to extinguish such cravings or at least try to gain control over them. That is, I might try to make my actions conform to my second-order desires. If I am successful in these endeavors, I have *freedom of the will*, which, according to Frankfurt, is the ability to will whatever I want to will. I am not simply led around by my first-order desires; my deeper, more personal, second-order desires are in control.

Frankfurt does not attempt to establish that persons are the ultimate causes of their second-order desires. It is only important that we are in control of our second-order desires and that our actions and first-order desires are organized in the right way. The focus is on alignment not origin of desires. There is a difference between having a responsible character and being responsible for one's character. In contrast to Frankfurt, Fischer requires *ownership*, not just identification.

Nonetheless, there is also a worry about ownership, expressed by Thomas Nagel: "A person can be morally responsible only for what he does; but what he does results from a great deal of what he does not do" (1976). Nagel offers this as a paradox of moral responsibility. What we do is a result of the character we have. We seem to have some influence on our present character but eventually, it seems, our character is influenced by factors that are external to ourselves and thus beyond our control.

Nagel's views have had a profound effect on Wolf, who presents a similar, more developed paradox:

> ... the agent's will is not wholly or deeply her own because the content of her will is completely determined by forces, people, and events external to herself. But if the content of the agent's will is not so determined – if her having the will she does is instead, in part, a result of random events, or if it is a matter of brute, inexplicable fact – this hardly seems to make her will more wholly or deeply her own. Indeed, recalling the case of the kleptomaniac, it may seem irrelevant whether the agent's will is controlled by something else or by nothing at all. (Wolf 1990)

For simplicity, let's identify one's character with the content of the agent's will, though I am not suggesting that Wolf makes this identification. As Wolf notes, even if our character is not completely determined we are no more responsible for our actions. What is crucial is that our character be determined by ourselves. This seems impossible. Eventually we seem to come across factors which are causally relevant to the development of our characters but which are external to ourselves.

Nagel suggests that this is also a problem about *genuine agency*, a problem about *causation* and causal chains. Initially, we might hold one responsible for his actions because he is the cause of his actions. But clearly he did what he did because he is the person that he is, because he has the particular character that he has, and because he is in the particular situation he is in. Why not, then, take the causal chain back further? Once we take this step, we realize that we must eventually appeal to events external to the agent, so long as the agent has a contingent and limited existence. How can anyone ever be responsible for his actions? These are the kinds of worries that were revealed in the manipulation argument (§ 4.2) and the ultimacy argument (§ 4.3). It is not certain that source theories can secure the kind of soucehood that is required for moral responsibility, especially if ultimate sourcehood is required.

For this reason and others, classical compatibilism is not dead yet. The hypothetical analysis has led to more sophisticated explanations of free will: possible worlds analyses of "can" (Lehrer 1976; Horgan 1979), contextualist treatments of "can" (Lewis 1976, 1979), and dispositional analyses of "able" (Vihvelin 2004). Possible worlds analyses are beyond the scope of this book but contextualism and dispositionalism deserve some attention.

Recall the *relevant facts account*, noted above. Contextualism is a *semantic* theory, that is a theory about the meaning and truth of *sentences*, not propositions. Thus, we should first define the relevant facts account in terms of sentences: "*S* is able to do otherwise" is true only if *S*'s doing otherwise is compossible with the relevant set of facts (Lewis 1976 and 1979). Call sentences of the form "*S* is able to do *a*" **ability-ascribing sentences**. **Contextualism** is the view that the truth-conditions of ability-ascribing sentences vary according to the context in which those sentences are uttered (Unger 1984; DeRose 1992, 1999). Contextualist theories are currently in vogue in epistemology, particularly in the analysis of "know" and its cognates as they occur in sentences like "Joe knows that he has a head." Contextual analyses of "can," "free action," and other terms relevant to the free will debate have also been given.[9]

David Lewis offers a contextualist analysis of "can" in response to the grandfather paradox (§ 1.3). Recall Tim, who travels back in time in an attempt to kill Grandfather prior to the birth of Tim's parents. Tim will fail to kill him, since doing so would lead to contradictions, but *can* Tim kill his grandfather? Lewis writes:

> We have this seeming contradiction: "*Tim doesn't, but can, because he has what it takes*" versus "*Tim doesn't, and can't, because it's logically impossible to change the past.*" I reply that there is no contradiction. Both conclusions are true, and for the reasons given. They are compatible because "can" is equivocal. (1976, 77)

Here is a helpful quotation from Ted Sider.

> Lewis's idea is that a statement attributing ability, like "Tim can kill Grandfather," is ambiguous. The statement means "Tim's killing Grandfather is compossible with a certain set of facts," but the relevant set of facts may vary from one context of utterance to another. When we say that Tim can kill Grandfather because he has what it takes, we mean that

his killing Grandfather is compossible with a certain set of facts that includes only relatively 'local' facts about the killing situation; when we say that Tim can't kill Grandfather because Grandfather is Tim's grandfather, we mean that Tim's killing Grandfather isn't compossible with a more inclusive set of facts that includes the fact that Grandfather survived his youth and helped produce Tim. (1997, 143)

According to Lewis and Sider, the truth-conditions of ability-ascribing sentences vary according to the context in which those sentences are uttered. Thus, an utterance of the sentence "Tim can kill Grandfather" may be true in ordinary contexts, where only local facts are under consideration, yet false in philosophical contexts, where global facts are taken into consideration. On this way of understanding contextualism, "can" always *means* the same thing. What varies from context to context – if contextualism is true – are the set of facts that are counted as relevant, not the meaning of "can" (Perry 1997; cf. Perry 2001, 17–18).

Contextualism is contrasted with Moore's view. Moore (1912) distinguishes between the hypothetical sense and the categorical sense of "able" or "can." The latter is picked out by the incompatibilist criterion; the former is usually identified with the hypothetical analysis: if S had wanted (or tried, etc.) to do otherwise, then S would have done otherwise. Moore holds that "can" has two distinct meanings and in doing so he distinguishes his position from the one held by the contextualist.

Contextualism is a compatibilist theory even though it endorses a variant of the incompatibilist criterion. Suppose that S does a. Could S have done otherwise? According to the contextualist, in ordinary contexts the answer is "Yes," since in those contexts we are only attentive to the local facts. If S's doing otherwise is compossible with that set of facts, S could have done otherwise. This is so even if determinism is true and S's doing otherwise is not compossible with all of the facts about the broad past. It concedes that the same act may be both free and determined, so contextualism is a compatibilist theory. That his actions are determined is not enough to render an agent unfree but if our attention shifts to a wider set of facts – for instance, if we suddenly reflect upon facts about the broad past and the truth of determinism

– the context changes, as well, and in this new context an utterance of the very same ability-ascribing sentence comes out false. Hence, the contextualist accepts a version of the incompatibilist criterion: If *S*'s doing *a* is not compossible with the facts about the broad past *and these facts are not properly ignored*, then *S* cannot do *a* (Hawthorne, 2001, 74).

Dispositionalism is the view that free will is a set of *dispositional powers*, powers like flammability, solubility, and fragility. Interestingly, dispositional powers were once given conditional analyses similar to the hypothetical analysis. These analyses were subject to counterexamples, as well. For instance, one might contend that "X is fragile" means "X would break if it were struck." Yet suppose that a sorcerer casts a spell that renders a glass unbreakable should it be struck (Martin 1994). The glass can never be broken, so its dispositional power of fragility can never be manifested. Nonetheless it seems that unless and until the glass is struck, it has the dispositional power of fragility. The fragility of the glass is a **finkish disposition**, one that "would vanish immediately, on being put to the test" (Vihvelin 2004, 435). Given the possibility of finkish dispositions, no conditional analysis of dispositional powers will work. Or so it seems.

David Lewis (1997) provides a *revised* conditional analysis of dispositional powers that attempts to get around the possibility of finkish dispositions. This is a controversial issue but what's more important, given our interests, is that Kadri Vihvelin (2004) uses Lewis's analysis to provide her own dispositionalist view of free will. According to *dispositionalism*, free will is a set of dispositional powers. Vihvelin writes: "To have free will is to have the ability to make choices on the basis of reasons and to have this ability is to have a bundle of dispositions" (2004, 429). Like hypothetical ability, dispositional powers are perfectly compatible with determinism. After all, it's not as if things would cease to be flammable were determinism true. Furthermore, if Vihvelin's theory works, it also provides a response to Frankfurt cases. In Frankfurt cases, the agent's ability to do otherwise is a finkish disposition, so the ability can never be manifested. But it doesn't follow that the agent lacks the ability to do otherwise.

Two criticisms of dispositionalism are worth noting. Randy Clarke (2009) notes that dispositions can always be masked. In the case of **masked dispositions**, an object is prevented from manifesting its dispositional power without losing the disposition. Unlike finkish dispositions, masked dispositions never vanish. On the other hand, not all abilities are such that they can be masked. Consider the *ability to act*. One might argue that if this ability cannot be manifested, then the agent lacks the ability. What would it mean to say that I had the masked disposition to act, if in fact I could never really act? This example shows that the ability to act and the ability to act otherwise are intimately related.

The second important criticism of dispositionism comes from van Inwagen and was noted earlier (§ 2.4): "The concept of a causal [or dispositional] power or capacity would seem to be the concept of an invariable disposition to react to certain determinate changes in the environment in certain determinate ways, whereas the concept of an agent's power to act would seem not to be the concept of a power that is dispositional or reactive, but rather the concept of a power to *originate* changes in the environment (1983, 11)." Van Inwagen points to the importance of the *power to act*, not just the ability to do otherwise. The criticism is not decisive – who's to say that the power to act can't be a dispositional power? – but it is compelling.

Dispositionalism is fine if it is restricted to cognitive capacities. But what about understanding the *power to act* as a dispositional power? Suppose that the power to act is not explicable in terms of dispositional powers. What should the compatibilist do? I think that the compatibilist should do just what the incompatibilist does: accept that the power to act is essential to free will but admit that it is an *unanalyzable primitive power*. Free will is a set of active powers and cognitive capacities. The latter are explicable in terms of dispositional powers but the power to act is an unanalyzable primitive, meaning it is not explicable in terms of other concepts.

5.4 Alternative Views

Peter van Inwagen's views are as interesting as they are complex. He holds a classical incompatibilist view of free will but beyond that van Inwagen is difficult to categorize. He is the creator of some of the best and most powerful formal versions of the consequence argument (§§ 3.1–3.2). Yet he is equally critical of libertarian views of free will (§ 3.3) and he is no fan of the libertarian agency theory (§ 3.3). Even if we have free will, **restrictivism** – the view that "one has precious little free will, that rarely, if ever, is anyone able to do otherwise than he in fact does" (1989, 405) – is likely true, so our free acts are few and far between. No one said that explaining free will was going to be easy.

Van Inwagen (1998) suggests that we might lack the cognitive skills needed to solve the free will problem, which would explain its persistence. Some believe that this commits him to **mysterianism**, the view that the problem of free will is ultimately inexplicable. On the one hand, the consequence argument is very compelling. But the *Mind* argument is equally compelling. Nonetheless, it seems that we have free will. Van Inwagen supposes that it is the *Mind* argument that is at fault, though its precise fault is unknown. Still, few philosophers can articulate the puzzles and paradoxes of free will – as well as the available solutions – as well as van Inwagen.

A related and equally interesting view is Al Mele's **agnosticism** about the problem of free will and determinism. He acknowledges the strength of the zygote argument yet regards it as inconclusive (Mele 1995, 190–191; Mele 2006, 188–195). Similar comments apply to the role that luck plays in the *Mind* argument (2006, Ch. 3). *Agnostic autonomism* provides the best support of the free will thesis, according to Mele, for the disjunction of compatibilism or incompatibilism is more probable than either theory on its own.

Revisionism, developed and defended by Manuel Vargas (Fischer, Kane, Pereboom, and Vargas 2007), is difficult to define. Here is a brief synopsis, which is discussed in more detail below. The revisionist thinks that the folk understanding of *free will* is essentially incompatibilist yet also thinks that libertarianism is flawed because it is incoherent (§ 4.3), or unwarranted (§ 3.3), or empirically false (Pereboom 2001; Fischer, Kane, Pereboom, and Vargas, 2007, 111–114). Perhaps the compatibilist has something better to offer. Thus, we are in need of a conceptual revolution, a revision of the concept of *free will*.

In order to better understand revisionism, consider P. F. Strawson's distinction between *descriptive* and *revisionary metaphysics*. Strawson writes: "Descriptive metaphysics is content to describe the actual structure of our thought about the world, revisionary metaphysics is concerned to produce a better structure" (Strawson 1990). Similarly, for Vargas, accounts of free will can be divided into *descriptive* and *revisionary accounts*. **Descriptive accounts** of free will are committed to *conceptual analysis*. As Vargas understands this, they are concerned with describing how we "think and talk about free will." **Revisionary accounts** of free will are *normative*, they tell us how we should think. **Revisionism**, according to Vargas, is "the view that what we ought to believe about free will and moral responsibility is different than what we tend to think about these things" (127). Thus, technically speaking, revisionism is a revisionary account yet what makes Vargas's theory so interesting is that he begins with results from *descriptive metaphysics* and argues for revisionism on this basis.

For these reasons, Vargas provides both a *diagnostic account* and a *prescriptive account* in defense of revisionism. The former is "an account of free will that attempts to reflect how we tend to think about and talk about free will" but the latter "aims to tell us how we ought to think about it" (129). The diagnostic account suggests that "common sense is incompatibilist" (131) and we have a "libertarian self-conception" of *free will* (128). Vargas supports this claim with three sorts of considerations (131).

First, Vargas thinks that the persuasiveness of arguments for incompatibilism, most notably the consequence argument (§§ 3.1–2) suggests an incompatibilist sense of "ability," something that satisfies the incompatibilist criterion. As Vargas writes: "we see ourselves as having genuine, robust alternative possibilities" (128). Second, data from *experimental philosophy* suggests that our common sense intuitions are incompatibilist. Third, it is supported by "reflections on cultural and social history" (128). For instance, our concept of *free will*, either the classical or source understanding, is connected with our attitudes about moral responsibility (128; 136). Most people believe that persons are morally responsible for their actions. Thus, our conception of *free will* is connected with a range and assortment of social policies.

Revisionism is a provocative and compelling view yet a few critical points are worth noting. For one thing, it is not clear that our self-conception of free will is libertarian. It is far from clear that experimental data suggests that the folk conception of *free will* is libertarian (Nahmias, Morris, Nadelhoffer, and Turner 2005). More likely than not, our self-conception of *free will* is incoherent, reflecting both compatibilist and incompatibilist assumptions. This would explain why the problem of free will is perennial and unlikely to go away anytime soon.

Keith Lehrer (1976) describes the problem of free will and determinism as a conflict between *practice* and *theory*. On the one side are our practical needs, which require that we regard others as free and responsible persons. This is the basis of ethics, law, and a variety of social practices. Yet we also have theoretical concerns about the world. We attempt to understand it, to construct theories about it, and to make predictions on the basis of these theories. This is the basis of science and metaphysics. It is likely that, if we press people on practical issues, their commitment to freedom surfaces but, when we press them on theoretical issues, their commitment to determinism comes out. It is unlikely that this conflict, which arises when we try to understand ourselves as things in the world, will go away any time soon.

Suppose we concede that the folk conception of *free will* is a libertarian conception. Where does that get us? It is a mistake to think that all descriptive accounts of free will aim to describe some particular metaphysical account, the account of the "folk." Recall Strawson's quote: "Descriptive metaphysics is content to describe the actual structure of our thought about the world" (Strawson 1990). The aim is not to *describe the world*, to say whether the kind of free will in the world is libertarian or compatibilist. The aim is to *describe our thoughts about the world*. And our thoughts about the world cannot be settled by consensus, for they include thoughts shared by both the compatibilist and the incompatibilist. Strawson lists Aristotle and Kant as paradigmatic descriptive metaphysicians. These are system builders, attempting to delineate the scope and limits of human thought.

Both had their views about free will, though in each case exactly which view is held is debatable. Rather than merely tell us what free will is, both provide a *taxonomy*, a way to understand the various theories and debates surrounding free will. This is not really a criticism of revisionism – revisionists can accommodate these concerns – but they are points worth mentioning.

Peter F. Strawson's criticisms of free will skepticism (1962, 1985) are part of a broader naturalism that is intended to respond to other skeptical worries, as well. Among the other forms of skepticism that Strawson considers are threats to "the existence of the external world, i.e. of physical objects or bodies; our knowledge of other minds; the justification of induction; the reality of the past" (1985, 2–3). Thus, some general comments are in order before we discuss Strawson's response to free will skepticism.

Strawson distinguishes between two kinds of naturalism. **Reductive naturalism** does not allow for the existence of anything "which is not ultimately reducible to or explicable in terms of the natural sciences" (1998a, 168). Strawson writes:

> An exponent of some subvariety of reductive naturalism in some particular area of debate may sometimes be seen, or represented, as a kind of skeptic in that area: say, a moral skeptic or a skeptic about the mental or about abstract entities or about what are called "intensions". (1985, 2)

Strawson continues:

> It is reductive naturalism which holds that the naturalistic or objective view of human beings and human behavior undermines the validity of moral attitudes and reactions and displays moral judgment as no more than a vehicle of illusion. (1985, 43)

Reductive naturalists are moral skeptics. Not surprisingly, Strawson rejects reductive naturalism in favor of his own variety: nonreductive naturalism. **Nonreductive naturalism** "provides for a richer conception of the real, making room, for example, for morality and moral responsibility, for sensible qualities as genuinely characterizing physical things, for determinate meanings, meaning-rules, and universals – all as we ordinarily conceive them" (1998a, 168).

According to nonreductive naturalism, arguments for skepticism – whether it is epistemological skepticism or some metaphysical variety like free will skepticism – "are not to be met with argument" but "are simply to be neglected" (Strawson 1985, 13). Strawson continues:

> To try to meet the skeptic's challenge, in whatever way, by whatever style of argument, is to try to go further back. If one is to begin at the beginning, one must refuse the challenge as our naturalist refuses it. (1985, 24–5)

Implicit in this non-response to the skeptic is the suggestion that there are no adequate replies available. Thus, Strawson's view is a kind of *concessive response* to the skeptical challenge.[10] Strawson writes: "the point has been, not to offer a rational justification of the belief in external objects and other minds or the practice of induction, but to represent skeptical arguments and rational counter-arguments as equally idle – not senseless, but idle – since what we have here are original, natural, inescapable commitments which we neither choose nor could give up" (1985, 28; cf. 1998b, 242).

Strawson's concession does not result in a victory for the skeptic since skeptical arguments have no lasting effect on us. We continue to act as if some beliefs are true independent of our inability to provide an adequate response to the skeptical arguments against them. Skeptical arguments are, thus, "idle" and have no effect on our beliefs. Yet it isn't just the skeptical arguments that are idle, for "arguments on both sides are idle" (1985, 29).

Consider, for instance, Strawson's comments in response to skepticism about the past. Strawson writes:

> ... belief in the reality and determinateness of the past is as much part of that general framework of beliefs to which we are inescapably committed as is the belief in the existence of physical objects and the practice of inductive belief-formation ... All form part of our mutually supportive natural metaphysics. (1985, 29)

According to nonreductive naturalism, we simply believe in the existence of the past, the reality of the external world, and our inductive practices for "we have an original non-rational commitment which sets the bounds within which, or the stage upon which, reason can effectively operate, and within which the question of the rationality or irrationality, justification or lack of justification, of this or that particular judgment or belief can come up" (1985, 39). Ludwig Wittgenstein (1969) calls these beliefs "the inherited background against which I distinguish between true and false" (§ 94) and "the substratum of all my inquiring and asserting" (§ 162) (cf. Strawson 1985, 15). Strawson claims that such a background is "internal to the structure of all thinking, so that the attempt to question it, which is tantamount to an attempt to reject our conceptual scheme in its entirety, leaves us without the resources for any coherent thought at all" (1998d, 291).

One might attempt to solve the problem of the external world by providing a rational justification that takes the form of an argument, similar to G. E. Moore's famous proof of the external world (cf. Wright 2004).

PREMISE   Here is a hand.

CONCLUSION   An external world exists.[11]

A rational justification need not take the form of an explicit argument but what is essential is that something is a **rational justification** for a belief *p* only if it also provides a reason to think that *p* is likely to be true. In contrast, a **pragmatic justification** for *p* provides a reason for believing that *p* without providing a reason to think that *p* is likely to be true.

Pascal's wager is an excellent example of a pragmatic justification for belief in the existence of God. Pascal offers reasons for believing in the existence of God but those reasons do not suggest that it is likely that God exists. It might be the case that each of us would be better off believing in the existence of God, for the benefits of belief far outweigh the dangers of disbelief. Yet that does not render it more probable than not that God exists.

Strawson is concerned to explain the appropriateness of certain "natural beliefs" – for instance, the belief that we know some things, that the external world exists, that other minds exist, that the future will be like the past, that the past exists or at least did exist, that we have free will, that we are morally responsible for our actions.[12] Yet Strawson provides neither a rational justification nor a pragmatic justification for natural beliefs. His claim is not that we *should* accept them but merely that we *do* and that we do so independent of reasoning or argument. Natural beliefs are appropriate because of the cental role that they play in our overall system of beliefs.

Strawson's criticisms of incompatibilism and free will skepticism do not render the free will thesis more probable than not. Strawson's response to the free will skeptic is part of a more general strategy toward skeptical arguments. Strawson writes:

> The correct way with the professional skeptical doubt is not to attempt to rebut it with argument, but to point out that it is idle, unreal, a pretense; and then the rebutting arguments will appear as equally idle; the reasons produced in those arguments to justify induction or belief in the existence of body are not, and do not become, *our* reasons for these beliefs; there is no such thing as *the reasons for which we hold* these beliefs. We simply cannot help accepting them as defining the areas within which the questions come up of what beliefs we should rationally hold on such-and-such a matter. (1985, 19–20)

Strawson's nonreductive naturalism reveals a rhetorical advantage for the compatibilist. For we are going to hold people morally responsible and we are going to suppose that our actions are up to us regardless of philosophical arguments to the contrary. This is why the questions raised in this book will remain long after the pages turn to dust.

Lastly, there is **metacompatibilism**, the view that compatibilism is preferred over incompatibilism for metaphilosophical reasons. Strawson is a metacompatibilist and like his view, our metacompatibilism offers an overall response to the skeptic. Recall that a *skeptic* is someone who doubts what others believe to be true yet doubt comes in degrees. The agnostic and the atheist have their doubts about God but the latter's doubts are more severe. The atheist is a *metaphysical skeptic*, not just an epistemological one. The agnostic has doubts, to be sure, but they are mere doubts, not explicit denials. The agnostic is an *epistemological skeptic*.

Both forms of skepticism have global and local varieties. *Global epistemological skepticism* is the thesis that no one knows anything. Few philosophers endorse *global metaphysical skepticism* – the view that nothing exists – but varieties of *local metaphysical skepticism* remain popular, such as atheism and free will skepticism.

As was noted, arguments for (global) epistemological skepticism and (metaphysical) free will skepticism bear important formal features. More specifically, the most popular version of the argument for epistemological skepticism (DeRose 1999) is structurally similar to the consequence argument (§§ 3.1–2). Both arguments employ closure principles. In the case of the consequence argument, there are no-choice transfer principles like principles (β) and (β'). In addition, both arguments hinge on the meanings of slippery modal terms like "able" and "know." Because of these similarities, each argument is amenable to similar replies. For each argument, there are common sense replies and sophisticated analyses; there is the possibility that key terms – "able," "can," and "know," and their cognates – are ambiguous; there is the relevant facts account and its complement, the relevant alternatives account; there are contextualist analyses of each; there are metaphilosophical responses, as well, both to the consequence argument and the argument for epistemological skepticism.

Now it might turn out in each case that the response to the consequence argument is worse than the response to the argument for epistemological skepticism. But a likelier thesis is that for every response to the argument for epistemological skepticism, there is a formally analogous response to the consequence argument that is equally plausible. If so, we have the following compelling argument.

- For every response to the argument for epistemological skepticism there is a response to the consequence argument that is equally plausible.
- If one adopts epistemological skepticism, then one should reject free will skepticism as just so much dogma.
- Therefore, there is no good reason to deny that we have free will.

The second premise should be obvious: the epistemological skeptic is an agnostic about free will, not a free will denier. The first premise is debatable but if it can be established, it would show that there is no good reason to endorse free will skepticism.

5.5   Final Thoughts

Smilansky (2001) thinks that the nonreductive naturalist response to free will skepticism is complacent. Yet nonreductive naturalism is the last line of defense. After critical analysis, several theories of free will are left standing. Balaguer (2010) has given a compelling indeterminist theory of freedom and has argued persuasively that there is no reason to deny that the kind of indeterminism needed for libertarian free will is true. Even Pereboom concedes that the agency theory is possible. Related compatibilist theories are in the offering, as well (Fischer 1994; Lehrer 2004; Vihvelin 2004).

Ultimately, it comes down to the arguments for free will skepticism (§ 3.4) and skepticism about moral responsibility (§ 4.3), which are themselves dependent upon the arguments for incompatibilism (§§ 3.1–2) and incompatibilism about moral responsibility (§§ 4.1–2). There is no denying that these arguments have a lot of intuitive support but when you look closely at them, they are not decisive. Hence, there is no compelling reason to adopt either incompatibilism or incompatibilism about moral responsibility. It follows that there is no compelling reason to adopt either free will skepticism or skepticism about moral responsibility. Maybe we don't have free will. Maybe we're not morally responsible for anything. Nonetheless, there is no compelling reason to think either of these claims is true.

Further Reading

Mele (1997b) and Clarke (2008) provide nice general introductions to the philosophy of action. Libertarian theories of free will are offered by Ginet (1990), Kane (1996), O'Connor

(2000), Clarke (2003), and Balaguer (2010). Important agent-causal views include: Chisholm (1964), Clarke (1996), and Markosian (2002). Compelling arguments for free will skepticism are given by Double (1996), Strawson (1986), Honderich (1988, 2002), Smilansky (2000), and Pereboom (2001). Frankfurt (1988), Lehrer (1990), and Fischer (1994) offer the best versions of compatibilism to date.

Notes

1 Free Will

1 Keith Lehrer notes, in correspondence, that often we make unreflective choices, so our choices may not always be actions. Gary Watson (1987a) persuasively argues that free will is not free action.
2 Thanks to Kevin Timpe.
3 Mark Balaguer offered this terminology in correspondence.
4 Thanks to Scott Sehon, Kevin Timpe, and Manuel Vargas for pressing me on this. See Timpe (2008) for an alternative taxonomy.
5 Thanks to V. Alan White.
6 Thanks to Jonathan Westphal for helping me with this section.
7 Determinism is regarded as a *symmetrical* thesis, since all known laws of physics are symmetrical. Thus, a complete description of any state of the universe together with the laws of nature entails each and every true proposition (see van Inwagen 1983, 65; Earman 2004; Bishop 2006; Hoefer 2010). This added complexity is ignored.
8 The problem of free will is immune to ontological solutions (see § 3.3).
9 Ted Honderich (1988, 2002) is still a determinist. See below (§ 5.2).

2 Moral Responsibility

1 Thanks to Manuel Vargas for pointing this out.
2 Thanks to Kadri Vihvelin.
3 In Frankfurt's original example, "Jones" was "Jones₄."

3   The Problem of Free Will

1   The first argument was initially called the "main argument" (van Inwagen 1975).

4   Moral Responsibility: Incompatibilism and Skepticism

1   Actually, van Inwagen (1980, 1983) uses 'N' for the non-responsibility operator as well as the no-choice operator. The 'NR' operator is from Widerker (2002, 317).
2   This example is called "tax evasion (2)" by Pereboom (2003).
3   It is difficult to specify these conditions more precisely. For the sake of brevity, I assume the truth of causalism, where *causalism* is the view that "an event's being an action depends upon how it is caused" and actions are causally explained in terms of "such psychological or mental items as beliefs, desires, intentions, and related events" (Mele 1997b, 2–3; cf. § 5.1). I contend that a similar set of conditions may be offered that would satisfy noncausal theories of action, as well, but I do not discuss the matter here. For examples of noncausal theories, see Ginet 1990 and Sehon 2005. Also, for convenience, I'm assuming that, in any genuine Frankfurt case, there are only two possible causal chains: c_1 and c_2. Really, only two *types* of causal chains are possible.
4   Thanks to Scott Sehon.

5   Free Will Theories

1   Thanks to Harry Silverstein for suggesting this.
2   Timpe (2008) uses this as a reason to call Kane a source theorist, not a classical theorist. I concede that Timpe's taxonomy is no worse than the one I am using. Nonetheless, on my taxonomy Kane holds the classical view of free will since he endorses something like the **classical freedom (with tracing) condition**: a person is morally responsible for an act only if he is or was able to do otherwise (§ 2.2). See below.
3   Thanks to Bob Kane.
4   Compatibilism and incompatibilism are, by definition, **contradictories**: if one is true, the other is false. Honderich questions this taxonomy and suggests that compatibilism and

incompatibilism are **contraries**: they can't both be true but they can both be false.

5   Thanks to Saul Smilansky.

6   Moore uses the term "can" or its cognates but it turns out that "can" is ambiguous in ways that Moore did not anticipate, so "able" is used instead (van Inwagen 2008).

7   Moore's analysis: "we could have done otherwise" means "(1) that we . . . *should* have *acted* differently, if we had chosen to; (2) that similarly we . . . should have *chosen* differently, *if* we had chosen so to choose; and (3) that it was . . . *possible* that we should have chosen differently, in the sense that no man could know for certain that we should *not* so choose" (1912, 94).

8   Thanks to Manuel Vargas.

9   Lewis (1976 and 1979) and Sider (1997) develop contextualist theories of ability terms. Hawthorne (2001) presents a contextualist theory of "free action." Unger (1984, 54–8) discusses both kinds of theories. Feldman (2004) offers compelling criticisms of contextualism.

10   For other concessive responses to skepticism, see DeRose and Warfield (1999, Part 5). For a discussion of these responses, see DeRose (1999, 19–22). The term 'concessive response' is DeRose and Warfield's but it fits Strawson well. In response to a criticism about his endorsement of Hume, Strawson writes: "Professor Black rightly emphasizes that Hume's skepticism is at least as strong as what I have chosen to call his naturalism. Indeed it is. Hume is surely right in holding that reason can never take us from his own chosen epistemological premises to a firmly grounded belief in the existence of body" (1998b, 242).

11   At least one of Strawson's critics (Sosa 1998, 366–367) interprets him as providing a similar rational justification of our belief in the external world. See below and Strawson 1998e for replies to this interpretation.

12   The term 'natural belief' is not Strawson's. It comes from the Hume literature, specifically Norman Kemp Smith. Indeed, it is worth noting that Strawson, citing Hume and Wittgenstein, questions "the appropriateness of the ordinary concepts of 'belief' and 'proposition' in this connection" (1998e, 370). I don't address this issue here.

References

Aristotle. 1985. *Nicomachean Ethics*, Book III. Trans. Terence Irwin. Selection reprinted in Pereboom 1997; page numbers refer to this latter edition.

Augustine. 1993. *On Free Choice of the Will*. Indianapolis: Hackett.

Balaguer, Mark. 2010. *Free Will as an Open Scientific Problem*. Cambridge, MA: MIT Press.

Beebee, Helen, and Alfred Mele. 2002. "Humean Compatibilism." *Mind* 111: 201–223.

Bennett, Jonathan. 1984. *A Study of Spinoza's Ethics*. Indianapolis: Hackett.

Berofsky, Bernard. 2003. "Classical Compatibilism: Not Dead Yet!" In McKenna and Widerker 2003.

Bishop, Robert C. 2006. "Determinism and Indeterminism." In *Encyclopedia of Philosophy*, 2nd edn., editor in chief, D. M. Borchert. Farmington Hills, MI: Macmillian Reference.

Boethius. 2001. *The Consolation of Philosophy*, trans. Joel C. Relihan. Indianapolis: Hackett.

Brueckner, Anthony. 2008. "Retooling the Consequence Argument." *Analysis* 68: 10–13.

Campbell, C. A. 1951. "Is 'Freewill' a Pseudo-Problem?" *Mind* 60: 441–465.

———. 1957. *On Selfhood and Godhood*. London: George Allen and Unwin.

Campbell, Joseph Keim. 1997. "A Compatibilist Theory of Alternative Possibilities." *Philosophical Studies* 88: 319–330.

———. 1999. "Descartes on Spontaneity, Indifference, and Alternatives." In *New Essays on the Rationalists*, ed. Rocco J. Gennaro and Charles Huenemann. Oxford: Oxford University Press.

———. 2005. "Compatibilist Alternatives." *Canadian Journal of Philosophy* 35: 387–406.

———. 2006. "Farewell to Direct Source Incompatibilism." *Acta Analytica* 21.4: 36–49.

———. 2007. "Free Will and the Necessity of the Past." *Analysis* 67: 105–111.

———. 2008a. "Touchdowns, Time, and Truth." In *Football and Philosophy*, ed. Mike Austin. Lexington: University Press of Kentucky.

———. 2008b. "New Essays in the Metaphysics of Moral Responsibility." *Journal of Ethics* 12: 119–201.

———. 2010. "Incompatibilism and Fatalism: Reply to Loss." *Analysis* 70: 71–6.

Campbell, Joseph Keim, Michael O'Rourke, and David Shier, eds. 2004a. *Freedom and Determinism*. Cambridge: The MIT Press.

———. 2004b. "Freedom and Determinism: A Framework." In Campbell, O'Rourke, and Shier 2004a.

Campbell, Joseph Keim, Michael O'Rourke, and Harry Silverstein, eds. 2010a. *Action, Ethics, and Responsibility*. Cambridge: The MIT Press.

———. 2010b. "Action, Ethics, and Responsibility: A Framework." In Campbell, O'Rourke, and Silverstein 2010-a.

Casati, Roberto, and Achille Varzi. 2010. "Events." In *The Stanford Encyclopedia of Philosophy (Spring 2010 Edition)*, ed. Edward N. Zalta. http://plato.stanford.edu/archives/spr2010/entries/events/.

Chisholm, Roderick. 1964. "Human Freedom and the Self." The Lindley Lecture, 3–15. Department of Philosophy, University of Kansas. Reprinted in Pereboom 1997.

Clarke, Randolph. 1993. "Toward a Credible Agent Causal Account of Free Will." *Nous* 27, 191–203. Reprinted in O'Connor 1995; page numbers refer to this latter edition.

———. 1996. "Agent Causation and Event Causation in the Production of Free Action." *Philosophical Topics*: 24: 19–48. Excerpted in Pereboom 1997; page numbers refer to this latter edition.

———. 2003. *Libertarian Accounts of Free Will*. Oxford: Oxford University Press.

———. 2005. "On an Argument for the Impossibility of Moral Responsibility." *Midwest Studies in Philosophy* 29: 13–24.

———. 2008. "Incompatibilist (Nondeterministic) Theories of Free Will." In *The Stanford Encyclopedia of Philosophy (Fall 2008*

Edition), ed. Edward N. Zalta. http://plato.stanford.edu/archives/fall2008/entries/incompatibilism-theories/.

———. 2009. "Dispositions, Abilities to Act, and Free Will: The New Dispositionalism." *Mind* 118: 323–351.

Conee, Earl, and Theodore Sider. 2005. *Riddles of Existence.* Oxford: Oxford University Press.

David, Marian. 2009. "The Correspondence Theory of Truth." *The Stanford Encyclopedia of Philosophy (Fall 2009 Edition)*, ed. Edward N. Zalta. http://plato.stanford.edu/archives/fall2009/entries/truth-correspondence/.

Davidson, Donald. 1963. "Actions, Reasons, and Causes." *Journal of Philosophy* 60: 685–700. Reprinted in Davidson 1980 and Mele 1997a.

———. 1973. "Freedom to Act." Reprinted in Davidson 1980.

———. 1980. *Essays on Actions and Events.* Oxford: Clarendon Press.

Deutsch, David, and Michael Lockwood. 1994. "The Quantum Physics of Time Travel." *Scientific American.*

DeRose, K. 1992. "Contextualism and Knowledge Attributions." *Philosophy and Phenomenological Research* 52: 913–929.

———. 1999. "Introduction: Responding to Skepticism." In DeRose and Warfield 1999.

DeRose, Keith, and Ted A. Warfield, eds. 1999. *Skepticism: A Contemporary Reader.* New York and Oxford: Oxford University Press.

Double, Richard. 1996. *Metaphilosophy and Free Will.* New York: Oxford University Press.

Earman, John. 2004. "Determinism: What We Have Learned and What We Still Don't Know." In Campbell, O'Rourke, and Shier 2004a.

Einstein, Albert. 1920. *Relativity: The Special and General Theory.* New York: Henry Holt.

Eliot, T. S. 1935. "Burnt Norton," *Four Quartets* (1943). In *The Complete Poems and Plays* (1953). New York: Harcourt Brace and Company.

Fara, Michael. 2009. "Dispositions." *The Stanford Encyclopedia of Philosophy (Summer 2009 Edition)*, ed. Edward N. Zalta. http://plato.stanford.edu/archives/sum2009/entries/dispositions/.

Feinberg, Joel. 1970. *Doing and Deserving: Essays in the Theory of Responsibility.* Princeton: Princeton University Press.

Finch, Alicia, and Ted A. Warfield. 1998. "The *Mind* Argument and Libertarianism." *Mind* 107: 515–528.

Fischer, John Martin. 1982. "Responsibility and Control." *Journal of Philosophy* 89: 24–40. Reprinted in Fischer 1986a.

———, ed. 1986a. *Moral Responsibility*. Ithaca: Cornell University Press.

———. 1986b. "Introduction." In Fischer 1986a.

———, ed. 1989a. *God, Foreknowledge, and Freedom*. Stanford: Stanford University Press.

———. 1989b. "Introduction: God and Freedom." In Fischer 1989a.

———. 1994. *The Metaphysics of Free Will: An Essay on Control*. Oxford: Blackwell.

———. 1999. "Recent Work on Moral Responsibility." *Ethics* 110: 49–66. Excerpted in Kane 2002a.

———. 2004. "The Transfer of Nonresponsibility." In Campbell, O'Rourke, and Shier 2004.

Fischer, John Martin, Robert Kane, Derk Pereboom, and Manuel Vargas. 2007. *Four Views of Free Will*. Oxford: Blackwell.

Fischer, John Martin, and Mark Ravizza, eds. 1993a. *Perspectives on Moral Responsibility*. Ithaca: Cornell University Press.

———. 1993b. "Introduction." In Fischer and Ravizza 1993a.

———. 1998. *Responsibility and Control: A Theory of Moral Responsibility*. Cambridge: Cambridge University Press.

Fox, John. 1987. "Truthmaker." *Australasian Journal of Philosophy* 65: 188–207.

Frankfurt, Harry. 1969. "Alternate Possibilities and Moral Responsibility." *Journal of Philosophy* 66: 828–839. Reprinted in Fischer 1986a, Frankfurt 1988, and Pereboom 1997; page numbers refer to this Pereboom edition.

———. 1971. "Freedom of the Will and the Concept of a Person." *Journal of Philosophy* 68: 5–20. Reprinted in Frankfurt 1988 and Pereboom 1997.

———. 1982. "What We are Morally Responsible For." In *How Many Questions? Essays in Honor of Sidney Morgenbesser*, ed. Leigh S. Cauman, Issac Levi, Charles Parsons, and Robert Schwartz. Indianapolis: Hackett. Reprinted in Frankfurt 1988 and Fischer and Ravizza 1993; page numbers refer to this latter edition.

———. 1987. "Identification and Wholeheartedness." In Schoeman 1987. Reprinted in Frankfurt 1988 and Fischer and Ravizza 1993a; page numbers refer to the latter edition.

———. 1988. *The Importance of What We Care About*. Cambridge: Cambridge University Press.

Garrett, Don. 1991. "Spinoza's Necessitarianism." In *God and Nature in Spinoza's Metaphysics*, ed. Yirmiyahu Yovel. Leiden: E. J. Brill.

Ginet, Carl. 1966. "Might We Have No Choice?" In Lehrer 1966a.

———. 1989. "Reasons Explanation of Action: An Incompatibilist Account." *Philosophical Perspectives* 3: 17–46. Reprinted in O'Connor 1995 and Mele 1997a.

———. 1990. *On Action*. Cambridge: Cambridge University Press.

———. 1996. "In Defense of the Principle of Alternative Possibilities: Why I Don't Find Frankfurt's Argument Convincing." *Philosophical Perspectives* 10: 403–417.

———. 1997. "Freedom, Responsibility and Agency." *Journal of Ethics* 1: 374–380. Reprinted in Kane 2002a; page references are to this latter edition.

———. 2000. "The Epistemic Requirements for Moral Responsibility." *Philosophical Perspectives* 14: 267–277.

———. 2002. "Reasons Explanations of Action: Causalist Versus Noncausalist Accounts." In Kane 2002b.

———. 2008. "In Defense of a Non-causal Account of Reasons Explanations." *Journal of Ethics* 12: 229–237.

Glanzberg, Michael. 2009. "Truth." *The Stanford Encyclopedia of Philosophy (Spring 2009 Edition)*, ed. Edward N. Zalta. http://plato.stanford.edu/archives/spr2009/entries/truth/.

Grau, Christopher, ed. 1995. *Philosophers Explore* The Matrix. Oxford: Oxford University Press.

Hahn, Lewis Edwin, ed. 1998. *The Philosophy of P. F. Strawson*. Chicago and LaSalle, IL: Open Court.

Hasker, William. 1989. *God, Time and Knowledge*. Ithaca, NY: Cornell University Press. Important excerpts from this book are reprinted in Kane 2002a.

Hawking, Stephen W. 1996. "Wormholes and Time Travel." *The Illustrated A Brief History of Time*. Bantum Books.

Hawthorne, J. 2001. "Freedom in Context." *Philosophical Studies* 104: 63–79.

———. 2004. *Knowledge and Lotteries*. Oxford. Oxford University Press.

Hinchliff, Mark. 1996. "The Puzzle of Change." *Philosophical Perspectives* 10: 119–136.

Hobart, R. E. 1934. "Free Will as Involving Determinism and Inconceivable Without It." *Mind* 43: 1–27.

Hoefer, Carl. 2010. "Causal Determinism." In *The Stanford Encyclopedia of Philosophy (Spring 2010 Edition)*, ed. Edward N. Zalta. http://plato.stanford.edu/archives/spr2010/entries/determinism-causal/.

Honderich, Ted, ed. 1973. *Essays on Freedom of Action*. London: Routledge and Kegan Paul.

———. 1988. *A Theory of Determinism: The Mind, Neuroscience, and Life-Hopes*. Oxford: Clarendon Press. Reprinted in 1990 as the paperbacks: *Mind and Brain* (vol. 1) and *The Consequences of Determinism* (vol. 2).

———. 2002. *How Free Are You?*, 2nd edn. Oxford and New York: Oxford University Press.

———. 2004. "After Compatibilism and Incompatibilism." In Campbell, O'Rourke, and Shier 2004a.

Horgan, Terry. 1979. " 'Could', Possible Worlds, and Moral Responsibility." *Southern Journal of Philosophy* 17: 345–358.

Hume, David. 1975. *An Enquiry Concerning Human Understanding*, 3rd edn, L. A. Selby-Bigge, ed., and P. H. Nidditch, revised. Oxford: Oxford University Press.

James, William. 1956. "The Dilemma of Determinism." In *The Will to Believe and Other Essays*. New York: Dover.

Kane, Robert. 1996. *The Significance of Free Will*. Oxford: Oxford University Press.

———. 2001. "Free Will: Ancient Dispute, New Themes." In *Reason and Responsibility*, ed. Joel Feinberg and Russell Schaffer-Landau Wadsworth Publishers. Excerpted in Kane 2002a; page numbers refer to this latter edition.

———, ed. 2002a. *Free Will*. Oxford: Blackwell.

———, ed. 2002b. *The Oxford Handbook of Free Will*. Oxford: Oxford University Press.

———. 2004. "Agency, Responsibility, and Indeterminism: Reflections on Libertarian Theories of Free Will." In Campbell, O'Rourke, and Shier 2004a.

———. 2005. *A Contemporary Introduction to Free Will*. New York and Oxford: Oxford University Press.

Kapitan, Tomis. 2002. "A Master Argument for Incompatibilism?" In Kane 2002b.

Kretzmann, Norman. 1966. "Omniscience and Immutability." *Journal of Philosophy* 63: 409–421.

Lehrer, Keith. 1966a. *Freedom and Determinism*, New York: Random House.

———. 1966b. "An Empirical Disproof of Determinism?" In Lehrer 1966a. Reprinted in Lehrer 1990.

———. 1968. "Cans without Ifs." *Analysis* 29: 29–32.

———. 1976. " 'Can' in Theory and Practice: A Possible Worlds Analysis." In *Action Theory*, ed. Miles Brand and Douglas N. Walton. Dordrecht: D. Reidel. Reprinted as "A Possible Worlds Analysis of Freedom" in Lehrer 1990.

———. 1980. "Preferences, Conditionals and Freedom." In *Time and Cause: Essays Presented to Richard Taylor*, ed. Peter van Inwagen. Dordrecht: D. Reidel. Reprinted in Lehrer 1990.

———. 1990. *Metamind.* Oxford: Clarendon Press.

———. 2004. "Freedom and the Power of Preference." In Campbell, O'Rourke, and Shier 2004a.

Leibniz, Gottfried Wilhelm. 1704. *New Essays on Human Understanding.* From *Early Modern Philosophy*, ed. Jonathan Bennett. http://www.earlymoderntexts.com/

Levy, Neil M. 2002. *Sartre.* Oxford, UK: Oneworld Publications.

Lewis, David. 1976. "The Paradoxes of Time Travel." *American Philosophical Quarterly* 13, 145–52. Reprinted in Lewis 1986; page numbers refer to this latter edition.

———. 1981. "Are We Free to Break the Laws?" *Theoria* 47: 113–121. Reprinted in Lewis 1986.

———. 1983. *Philosophical Papers*, Volume I, Oxford: Oxford University Press.

———. 1986. *Philosophical Papers*, Volume II, Oxford: Oxford University Press.

———. 1997. "Finkish Dispositions." *The Philosophical Quarterly* 47: 143–158.

Locke, John. 1690. *An Essay Concerning Human Understanding.* Book II, Ch. 27 is reprinted in Perry 1975. From *Early Modern Philosophy*, ed. Jonathan Bennett. http://www.earlymoderntexts.com/

Loss, Roberto. 2009. "Free Will and the Necessity of the Present." *Analysis* 69: 63–69.

———. 2010. "Fatalism and the Necessity of the Present: Reply to Campbell." *Analysis* 70: 76–78.

Martin, C. B. 1994. "Dispositions and Conditionals." *The Philosophical Quarterly* 44: 1–8.

Maugham, W. Somerset. 1931. *The Collected Plays of W. Somerset Maugham.* London: William Heinemann Ltd.

———. 2002. "A Compatibilist Version of the Theory of Agent Causation." *Pacific Philosophical Quarterly* 80: 257–277.

Markosian, Ned. 2009. "Time." In *The Stanford Encyclopedia of Philosophy (Fall 2009 Edition)*, ed. Edward N. Zalta. http://plato.stanford.edu/archives/fall2009/entries/time/.

McKay, Thomas and David Johnson: 1996. "A Reconsideration of an Argument Against Compatibilism." *Philosophical Topics* 24, 113–22.

McKenna, Michael. 1998. "Does Strong Compatibilism Survive Frankfurt Counter-Examples?" *Philosophical Studies* 91, 259–64.

————. 2001. "Source Incompatibilism, Ultimacy, and the Transfer of Non-Responsibility." *American Philosophical Quarterly* 38: 37–51.

————. 2005. "Neo's Freedom Whoa!" In *Philosophers Explore the Matrix*, ed. Christopher Grau. Oxford: Oxford University Press.

————. 2008. "A Hard-line Reply to Pereboom's Four-Case Manipulation Argument." *Philosophy and Phenomenological Research* 77: 142–159.

McKenna, Michael, and David Widerker, eds. 2003. *Moral Responsibility and Alternative Possibilities: Essays on the Importance of Alternative Possibilities*. Burlington: Ashgate.

Mele, Alfred R. 1995. *Autonomous Agents: From Self-Control to Autonomy*. Oxford: Oxford University Press.

————, ed. 1997a. *The Philosophy of Action*. Oxford: Oxford University Press.

————. 1997b. "Introduction." In Mele 1997a.

————. 2006. *Free Will and Luck*. Oxford: Oxford University Press.

————. 2008. "Manipulation, Compatibilism, and Moral Responsibility." *Journal of Ethics* 12: 263–286.

Moore, G. E. 1912. *Ethics*. New York: Oxford University Press.

Nadler, Steven. 2009. "Baruch Spinoza." *The Stanford Encyclopedia of Philosophy (Winter 2009 Edition)*, ed. Edward N. Zalta. http://plato.stanford.edu/archives/win2009/entries/spinoza/.

Nagel, Thomas. 1976. "Moral Luck." *Aristotelian Society: Supplementary Volume* 50: 137–152.

————. 1986. *The View from Nowhere*. Oxford: Oxford University Press.

Nahmias, Eddy, Stephen Morris, Thomas Nadelhoffer, and Jason Turner. 2005. "Surveying Freedom: Folk Intuitions about Free Will and Moral Responsibility." *Philosophical Psychology* 18: 561–584.

Nelkin, Dana K. 2001. "The Consequence Argument and the *Mind* Argument," *Analysis* 61: 107–15.

O'Connor, Timothy, ed. 1995. *Agents, Causes, and Events: Essays on Indeterminism and Free Will*. Oxford: Oxford University Press.

————. 1996. "Why Agent Causation?" *Philosophical Topics* 24 (1996), 143–158. Reprinted in O'Connor 1995; page references to this latter edition.

————. 2000. *Persons and Causes: The Metaphysics of Free Will*. Oxford: Oxford University Press.

Parfit, Derek. 1971. "Personal Identity." *Philosophical Review* 80: 3–27. Reprinted in Perry 1975.

————. 1986. *Reasons and Persons*. Oxford: Oxford University Press.

Pereboom, Derk. 1994. Determinism *al Dente*. *Nous* 29: 21–45. Reprinted in Pereboom 1997; page numbers refer to this latter edition.

————, ed. 1997. *Free Will*. Indianapolis: Hackett Publishing Company.

————. 2000. "Alternate Possibilities and Causal Histories." *Philosophical Perspectives* 14: 119–137. Excerpted in Kane 2002a.

————. 2001. *Living Without Free Will*. Cambridge: Cambridge University Press.

————. 2003. "Source Incompatibilism and Alternative Possibilities." In McKenna and Widerker 2003.

————. 2006. "Is Our Conception of Agent-Causation Coherent?" *Philosophical Topics* 32: 275–286.

————. 2008. "A Compatibilist Account of the Epistemic Conditions on Rational Deliberation." *Journal of Ethics* 12: 287–306.

Perry, John, ed. 1975. *Personal Identity*. Berkeley and Los Angeles: University of California Press.

————. 1997. "Indexicals and Demonstratives." In *A Companion to the Philosophy of Language*, ed. B. Hale and C. Wright. Oxford: Blackwell.

————. 2001. *Reference and Reflexivity*. Stanford: CSLI Publications.

————. 2004. "Compatibilist Options." In Campbell, O'Rourke, and Shier 2004a.

Pike, Nelson. 1965. "Divine Omniscience and Voluntary Action." *Philosophical Review* 74: 27–46. Reprinted in Fischer 1989a.

Ravizza, Mark. 1994. "Semi-Compatibilism and the Transfer of Non-Responsibility," *Philosophical Studies* 75: 61–93.

Rice, Hugh. 2010. "Fatalism." In *The Stanford Encyclopedia of Philosophy (Winter 2010 Edition)*, ed. Edward N. Zalta. http://plato.stanford.edu/archives/win2010/entries/fatalism/.

Reid, Thomas. 1983. *Inquiry and Essays*, R. E. Beanblossom and K. Lehrer, eds. Indianapolis: Hackett Publishing Company.

Rosen, Gideon. 2004. "Skepticism about Moral Responsibility." *Philosophical Perspectives* 18: 295–311.

Russell, Paul. 1992. "Strawson's Way of Naturalizing Responsibility." *Ethics*: 102: 287–302.

————. 1995. *Freedom and Moral Sentiment: Hume's Way of Naturalizing Responsibility*. Oxford: Oxford University Press.

————. 2008a. "Free Will, Art and Morality." *Journal of Ethics* 12: 307–25.

————. 2008b. "Hume on Free Will." *The Stanford Encyclopedia of Philosophy (Fall 2008 Edition)*, ed. Edward N. Zalta. http://plato.stanford.edu/archives/fall2008/entries/hume-freewill/.

————. 2010. "Selective Hard Compatibilism." In Campbell, O'Rourke, and Silverstein 2010a.

Sartre, Jean-Paul. 1956. *Being and Nothingness*. Trans. Hazel E. Barnes. New York: Philosophical Library.

Schick, Theodore, Jr. 2002. "Fate, Freedom, and Foreknowledge." In The Matrix *and Philosophy*, ed. William Irwin. Peru, IL: Open Court.

Schoeman, Ferdinand, ed. 1987. *Responsibility, Character, and the Emotions: New Essays on Moral Psychology*. Cambridge: Cambridge University Press.

Sehon, Scott. 2005. *Teleological Realism: Mind, Agency, and Explanation*. Cambridge, MA: MIT Press.

Sider, Theodore. 1997. "A New Grandfather Paradox?" *Philosophy and Phenomenological Research* 57, 139–144.

————. 2001. *Four-Dimensionalism: An Ontology of Persistence and Time*. Oxford: Oxford University Press.

Smilansky, Saul. 2000. *Free Will and Illusion*. Oxford: Clarendon Press.

————. 2001. "Free Will: From Nature to Illusion." *Proceedings of the Aristotelian Society* 101: 71–95.

————. Forthcoming. "Free Will: Some Bad News." In Campbell, O'Rourke, and Silverstein forthcoming-a.

Smith, Barry. 1999. "Truthmaker Realism." *Australasian Journal of Philosophy* 77: 274–291.

Sommers, Tamler. 2007. "The Objective Attitude." *The Philosophical Quarterly*.

Spinoza, Benedict (or Baruch). 1677. *Ethics Demonstrated in Geometrical Order*. From *Early Modern Philosophy*, ed. Jonathan Bennett. http://www.earlymoderntexts.com/

Sripada, Chandra Sekhar. Manuscript. "The Case Against Manipulation Cases."

Strawson, Galen. 1986. *Freedom and Belief*. Oxford: Oxford University Press.

————. 2002. "The Bounds of Freedom." In Kane 2002b.

————. 2004. "Free Will." In *Routledge Encyclopedia of Philosophy*, ed. E. Craig. London: Routledge.

Strawson, Peter F. 1962. "Freedom and Resentment." *Proceedings of the British Academy* 48: 1–25. Reprinted in Pereboom 1997 and Fischer and Ravizza 1993a.

————. 1980. "P. F. Strawson Replies." In van Straaten 1980.

————. 1985. *Skepticism and Naturalism: Some Varieties*. London: Methuen.

————. 1990. *Individuals: An Essay in Descriptive Metaphysics*. London: Routledge.

————. 1998a. "Reply to Simon Blackburn." In Hahn 1998.

————. 1998b. "Reply to Andrew Black." In Hahn 1998.

————. 1998c. "Reply to David Pears." In Hahn 1998.

————. 1998d. "Reply to Hillary Putnam." In Hahn 1998.

————. 1998e. "Reply to Ernest Sosa." In Hahn 1998.

Stump, Eleonore. 1990. "Intellect, Will, and the Principle of Alternate Possibilities." In *Christian Theism and the Problems of Philosophy*, ed. Michael D. Beaty. Notre Dame, IN: University of Notre Dame Press. Reprinted in Fischer and Ravizza 1993a.

————. 1996. "Libertarian Freedom and the Principle of Alternative Possibilities." In *Faith, Freedom, and Rationality*, ed. Jeff Jordan and Daniel Howard-Snyder. Lanham, MD: Rowman and Littlefield.

————. 1999. "Dust, Determinism, and Frankfurt: A Reply to Goetz." *Faith and Philosophy* 16: 413–422.

————. 2003. "Moral Responsibility Without Alternative Possibilities." In Widerker and McKenna 2003.

Taylor, Richard. 1963. *Metaphysics*, 1st edn. Englewood Cliffs, NJ: Prentice-Hall.

————. 1992. *Metaphysics*, 4th edn. Englewood Cliffs, NJ: Prentice-Hall.

Timpe, Kevin. 2008. *Free Will: Sourcehood and Its Alternatives*. London: Continuum.

Unger, Peter. 1984. *Philosophical Relativity*. Oxford: Blackwell.

Vargus, Manuel. 2005. "The Trouble with Tracing." *Midwest Studies in Philosophy* 29: 269–291.

van Inwagen, Peter. 1975. "The Incompatibility of Free Will and Determinism." *Philosophical Studies* 27: 185–199. Reprinted in Pereboom 1997; page numbers refer to this latter edition.

————. 1978. "Ability and Responsibility." *Philosophical Review* 87: 201–224. Reprinted in Fischer 1986a; page numbers refer to this latter edition.

————. 1980. "The Incompatibility of Responsibility and Determinism." *Bowling Green Studies in Applied Philosophy* 2: 30–7. Reprinted in Fischer 1986a.

————. 1983. *An Essay on Free Will*. Oxford: Clarendon Press.

————. 1989. "When is the Will Free?" *Philosophical Perspectives* 3: 399–422. Reprinted in O'Connor 1995.

————. 1998. "The Mystery of Metaphysical Freedom." In *Metaphysics: The Big Questions*, ed. Peter van Inwagen and Dean Zimmerman. Oxford: Blackwell.

———. 2000. "Free Will Remains a Mystery." *Philosophical Perspectives* 14: 1–19. Reprinted in Kane 2002b; page numbers refer to this latter edition.

———. 2004. "Van Inwagen on Free Will." In Campbell, O'Rourke, and Shier 2004a.

———. 2008. "How to Think about the Problem of Free Will." *Journal of Ethics* 12: 327–341.

Van Straaten, Zak, ed. 1980. *Philosophical Subjects*. Oxford: Clarendon Press.

Vargas, Manuel. 2005. "The Trouble with Tracing." *Midwest Studies in Philosophy* 29: 269–91.

Vihvelin, Kadri. 1996. "What Time Travelers Cannot Do." *Philosophical Studies* 81: 315–330.

———. 2004. "Free Will Demystified: A Dispositional Account." *Philosophical Topics* 32: 427–450.

———. 2008. "Compatibilism, Incompatibilism, and Impossibilism." In *Contemporary Debates in Metaphysics*, ed. Theodore Sider, John Hawthorne, and Dean Zimmerman. Oxford: Blackwell.

———. Manuscript. "Classical Compatibilism and Commonsense."

Vilhauer, Ben. 2009. "Free Will Skepticism and Personhood as a Desert Base." *Canadian Journal of Philosophy* 39: 489–511.

Wallace, R. Jay. 1994. *Responsibility and the Moral Sentiments*. Cambridge, MA: Harvard University Press.

Warfield, Ted A. 1996. "Determinism and Moral Responsibility are Incompatible." *Philosophical Topics* 24: 215–226.

Watson, Gary. 1975. "Free Agency." *Journal of Philosophy* 72, 205–20. Reprinted in Fischer 1986a.

———. 1987a. "Free Action and Free Will." *Mind* 96: 145–172.

———. 1987b. "Responsibility and the Limits of Evil: Variations on a Strawsonian Theme." In Schoeman. Reprinted in Fischer and Ravizza 1993a.

Westphal, Jonathan. 2003. "A New Way with the Consequence Argument, and the Fixity of the Laws." *Analysis* 63: 208–212.

Widerker, David. 1987. "On an Argument for Incompatibilism." *Analysis* 47, 37–41.

———. 1995a. "Libertarian Freedom and the Avoidability of Decisions." *Faith and Philosophy* 12: 113–118.

———. 1995b. "Libertarianism and Frankfurt's Attack on the Principle of Alternative Possibilities." *The Philosophical Review* 104: 247–261.

———. 2000. "Frankfurt's Attack on the Principle of Alternative Possibilities: a Further Look." *Philosophical Perspectives* 14: 181–201.

———. 2002. "Farewell to the Transfer Argument." *Journal of Philosophy* 99: 316–324.

Widerker, David, and Michael McKenna, eds. 2003. *Moral Responsibility and Alternative Possibilities: Essays on the Importance of Alternative Possibilities.* Aldershot, UK: Ashgate Publishing Company.

Wilson, George. 2009. "Action." In *The Stanford Encyclopedia of Philosophy (Fall 2009 Edition)*, ed. Edward N. Zalta. http://plato.stanford.edu/archives/fall2009/entries/action/.

Wood, Allen. 1984. "Kant's Compatibilism." In *Self and Nature in Kant's Philosophy*, ed. Allen Wood. Ithaca: Cornell University Press.

Wolf, Susan. 1990. *Freedom Within Reason.* Oxford: Oxford University Press.

Wright, Chrispen. 2004. "Wittgensteinian Certainties." In *Wittgenstein and Scepticism*, ed. Denis McManus. London and New York: Routledge.

Zagzebski, Linda. 1991. *The Dilemma of Freedom and Foreknowledge.* New York, NY: Oxford University Press.

———. 2002. "Recent Work on Divine Foreknowledge and Free Will." In Kane 2002a.

———. 2008. "Foreknowledge and Free Will." In *The Stanford Encyclopedia of Philosophy (Fall 2008 Edition)*, ed. Edward N. Zalta. http://plato.stanford.edu/archives/fall2008/entries/free-will-foreknowledge/.

Zimmerman, Dean. Forthcoming. "Presentism and the Space-Time Manifold." In *The Oxford Handbook of Time*, ed. Craig Callender. Oxford: Oxford University Press

Zimmerman, Michael J. 1997. "Moral Responsibility and Ignorance." *Ethics* 107: 410–426.

Index